JOHN FORD

series edited and designed by Ian Cameron

JOHN FORD

PETER BOGDANOVICH

UNIVERSITY OF CALIFORNIA PRESS

University of California Press
Berkeley and Los Angeles

University of California Press, Ltd.
London, England

For Teepee-That-Walks

The career index (Part 5) was first researched by Polly Platt. Frances Doal transcribed the interview, and the manuscript was typed by Mae Woods who has since updated the information on Ford's career with new material from The American Film Institute Catalog and from Joseph McBride.

"A Meeting at Monument Valley" originally appeared in Pieces of Time (Esquire-Arbor House, 1973) and is included for the first time in this expanded edition. Some of the material used in the Introduction—though considerably rewritten—was published in Esquire as "The Autumn of John Ford" (April, 1964) and was later reprinted in that form in Pieces of Time. Part 4 appeared originally as "Taps for Mr. Ford" in New York Magazine (October, 1973). All this material is used with the kind permission of the publishers. My thanks go to all these people. And to John Ford, and his wife, Mary, and his daughter, Barbara.

P.B.

2 3 4 5 6 7 8 9 0

ISBN: 0–520–03498-8
Library of Congress Catalog Card Number:
77–77522

Printed in the United States of America

Stills by courtesy of Milton Luboviski (of the Larry Edmunds Bookshop, Hollywood), John Kobal, Kevin Brownlow, The National Film Archive, Columbia, Metro-Goldwyn-Mayer, RKO Radio, Republic, Twentieth Century-Fox, United Artists, Universal, Olive Carey, Gene Ringgold, Warner Bros.

Frontispiece: Ford (centre) with John Wayne on the island of Kauai for Donovan's Reef.

CONTENTS

INTRODUCTION: A MEETING AT MONUMENT VALLEY

The morning after I arrived on the *Cheyenne Autumn* location in Monument Valley (accompanied by Polly Platt), the unit publicity man met us for breakfast to ask—it seems he hadn't been notified—what was my assignment for *Esquire*. "John Ford," I said.

He turned ashen. "Oh, no."

"Yes," I said.

"Oh, no, no," he said again, and looked around nervously as though to make sure we hadn't been overheard. I asked what was the matter and, shakily, he tried to explain that Mr Ford never granted interviews, hated reporters, shunned publicity, loathed talking about his movies and was simply unapproachable by anyone. I got the rather clear impression that this aging and by now almost haggard fellow would rather be swallowed up by the earth than risk even the thought of mentioning to Mr Ford that I was anywhere within a thousand-mile radius.

I countered by saying that his employer, Warner Bros., had just paid for our trip from New York to Arizona and that they'd been fully informed of my assignment when they issued the tickets. (Actually, it had taken more pressure on *Esquire* to agree to the article than Warners; they weren't terribly interested in the idea, but John Ford had for years been among my most cherished directors and I was very anxious both to meet him and to watch him at work, so after much badgering from my end, the editor, Harold Hayes, capitulated.) Well, said the bedraggled p.r. man, we could watch from the sidelines for awhile but I wasn't to speak to Mr Ford or even come under his gaze. At the moment, agreeing to that seemed the only way to even set foot on the set, so I did.

For two days, with the unit publicist hovering at my elbow every moment, I followed the rules he'd set down. Mr Ford would, on frequent occasions, pull out a handkerchief and chew on it, which the publicist nervously informed me was a sign of his displeasure and irritation. I only discovered sometime later that this was nonsense since Mr Ford, if he is not smoking or chewing a cigar, is *always* chewing on a handkerchief—it is not a signal of anything except probably that he's trying to cut down on smoking.

On the first Sunday afternoon—the only day they didn't shoot—I accidentally came upon Jack Garfein (the director), who was there visiting his then wife, Carroll Baker; they were going riding. Garfein and I had a mutual friend, the late Gene Archer, who was with *The New*

2

York Times then, and I used this as an excuse to introduce myself. When he asked what on earth I was doing there, I told him.

"Does Jack Ford know you're here?" he said.

"No, that's my problem," and I told him the situation.

"Oh, for God's sake," he said, "that's ridiculous. He'd love to see you. I'll tell him you're here."

About four hours later, a jeep came roaring down from the hill where Ford and the stars bunked (the rest of the company stayed below in trailers, one of which we'd been allotted), and I heard Ray Kellogg, the second-unit director, loudly yelling out what I finally figured out was a rough approximation of my name. I ran over.

"You MacDonabitch?"

"Yup."

"The Old Man'd like you to join him for dinner—around six. O.K.?"

"O.K.!"

Everyone was already seated when we arrived but whoever was on Mr Ford's right (I was too flustered to remember) was moved so that I could sit there. He nodded a pleasant hello, pronounced my name correctly and said, "Serbian?"

I said yes as casually as possible but I was impressed. All my life people had always assumed the name was Russian or Polish or Czech or Hungarian; sometimes they guessed Yugoslav, but no one had ever pinned it down precisely on the first try. At this point, the co-producer of the film, one Bernard Smith (of whom there will be more shortly), made some remark to the director having to do with business. Ford scowled at him silently for a moment, then turned to me: "There's a word for what he just said."

I leaned in. "Yes?"

"*Govno,*" Ford said. The word is the Serbian equivalent for "shit."

For the next week or so, Mr Ford was more than cooperative with me on the set; he was, in his own gruff way, actively friendly. It was often cold on the location and Polly took to wearing an Indian blanket wrapped around her, prompting Ford to name her "Teepee-That-Walks." I was sporting a British suede hat which he evidently disliked, so one day he yelled "Wardrobe" and instructed them to give me a cavalry hat. He then fitted it on me himself, adjusting the brim trooper-style until it pleased him. "That's better'n that Goddamn thing you've been wearing."

Now, this attention he was lavishing on us was not making the producer happy, mainly I guess because there had arrived on the location a writer and a photographer from *Life*, whom Ford quite blithely either ignored or insulted. He used to refer to the writer as "that guy from *Life, Death* and *Fortune.*" Eventually, producer Smith (whom I'd also made the tactical error of not interviewing) must have decided something had to be done so I was informed, with much trembling and stammering by the publicist, that we would have to leave—tomorrow; our trailer, went the excuse, had to be used for arriving members of the company. Since I'd told Warners originally I would need at least two weeks to get the piece right and they had agreed, I was not a little upset and annoyed to be thrown out after barely a week. I asked if Mr Ford was aware of this request and got an evasive answer to the effect that Mr Smith had sent down the order. Finally I had a reason to talk to the producer, which I did, with small effect. He smoothly explained the supposed problem of space, at the same time getting in several bows for his "contributions" to the production.

That evening, as he was heading in for dinner, I told Mr Ford we would have to be leaving tomorrow and thanked him for his patience.

"Where ya goin'?" he asked. I explained the

space problems we'd been informed of and that I didn't want to impose on his hospitality or make any waves. "Oh, c'mon in and let's eat," he said and we did that. Shortly after we were seated, the producer arrived. Ford called him over politely. "Listen, Bernie," he said very reasonably, "you give Bogdanovich here my room and I'll double up with someone down below."

The producer turned an odd color. "Oh, no, Jack, we can't do that."

"No, that's all right," said Ford, still very evenly, "you just give 'em my room if there's not enough space and I'll double up."

"Jack, don't be—I mean, that's ridiculous—we—we can—we can work something else out."

"Oh, can you, Bernie? You think you can find some space for them?"

"Sure, I can, Jack, don't worry about it."

"Oh, thanks, Bernie." The producer started away with relief. Ford called after him. "But, listen, if there's any trouble, they can just use *my* room, you know." Smith waved back with a pained grin. Ford's expression turned finally to a scowl and he leaned over to me. "Stay as long as you want," he said.

Over the years, since the article was published, my relations with Mr Ford weren't always as amicable or easy; it was impossible to be his friend or his admirer and not get some of that waspish Irish tongue or a touch of what James Cagney has referred to as "malice." But he is one of the great men of the movies and among the few really fascinating people I have met. That article, this book (which cannibalizes some of this same material) and the feature-length documentary I made about his career taken separately or together do not begin to do justice to who he was or to what he achieved.

Still on page 3: Ford and Bogdanovich while Bogdanovich was shooting Directed by John Ford.

1 MY NAME'S JOHN FORD. I MAKE WESTERNS.

'Take everything you've heard,' says James Stewart, 'everything you've ever heard . . . and multiply it about a hundred times—and you still won't have a picture of John Ford.'

'He'll be comin' over that rise any second now,' Danny Borzage said, and he looked up the road again. He was a bearded, youthful old man dressed in the yellow and blue of a trooper in the U.S. Cavalry, 1878, and he was playing 'Greensleeves' on his accordion. It was a little past 8:30 in the morning in Monument Valley, the sun was warm but the wind was chilling. Most of the huge *Cheyenne Autumn* company were preparing for the first scenes of the day, but a couple stood around listening to the accordion. 'I always play for 'im when he—'

'Here he comes, Danny!' A white jeep-station wagon had just appeared over the rise. Borzage walked quickly to the side of the road; as the car came nearer, he began to play 'Bringing in the Sheaves,' and he kept playing it as the car came to a slow stop about thirty feet from him and a hush fell over the company.

John Ford sat in the front seat, peering out of the window through thick glasses, his left eye covered with a black patch. He wore an old broad-brimmed felt hat pulled low over the left side of his face—there was a tiny orange feather in the leather hatband—and he chewed on a short, unlit cigar.

The prop man came over and handed him a cup of coffee, which he sipped, staring silently through the windshield. Borzage played 'She Wore A Yellow Ribbon'. William Clothier (cinematographer) and Frank Beetson (wardrobe) got out of the car and stood next to the director's window; they were joined by Wingate Smith (first assistant director) and Ford's son, Patrick, who was in charge of the cavalry on the picture. A muted conference went on at the window. Borzage was playing 'The Wild Colonial Boy' as the group broke up, one by one, to carry out instructions; Beetson opened the car door.

Ford got out and stood looking around for a moment, one hand holding the cup, the other on the backside of his hip. He was thin, almost frail, but as he started toward the camera his movement was jaunty, both arms swinging, his body moving slightly from side to side—and suddenly you knew where John Wayne got his walk.

People moved out of the way as he approached. He had a stern Yankee face, almost

Still: Montalban in Cheyenne Autumn.

mean, with a small growth of white stubble on his hollowed cheeks; his eyes were pale blue. He was wearing a faded tan campaign jacket and a pair of loose-fitting khakis; there was an orange scarf tied around his neck, and the laces of his dark blue sneakers were untied. Borzage played 'We Will Gather at the River'. Ford passed a Navajo and moved his right hand in a kind of half salute. 'Yat'hey, shi'kis,' he said, and the man answered, 'Yat'hey.'

'We were making a picture,' says cameraman Joseph LaShelle, 'and the head of the studio sent his assistant down to the set to tell Ford he was a day behind schedule. "Oh," said Ford, very polite, "well, how many pages would you figure we shoot a day?" "About eight, I guess," the guy said. "Would you hand me the script," Ford said, and the guy handed it to him. He counted out eight pages that hadn't been shot yet, ripped them out, and handed them to the guy. "You can tell your boss we're back on schedule now," he said. And he

never did shoot those eight pages.'

For the first shot, Ford placed some of the mounted Indians in shadow and some in light; Sal Mineo (as a young Cheyenne) was to throw down his rifle in anger, leap to his horse and ride off. Ford stood alone, rubbing his hands together; the gold signet ring he wore on his left hand had a deep groove across the initials caused by the thousands of kitchen matches he had struck on it. There was a lot of noise going on. 'Wingate!' Ford called out. 'What is this? Strike? Mutiny?'

Smith spoke through a bullhorn. 'All right. Let's keep it down now. Please!' Ford was looking over the Indians. 'Manymules is not wearing his blanket in this scene,' he said to the script supervisor, 'he's carrying it in his hand.' There was a slight but distinct Maine accent in his speech. 'All right, has anybody else got a reason why we can't do this? If not, let's go.'

During a rehearsal of the dialogue, Ford spotted one of the young Navajos in the background grinning into the camera. He called him aside, made him bend down over his knee, and spanked him. The company laughed; the young man backed off, giggling, and Ford made a mock gesture as though to sock him.

The camera rolled. Mineo ran to his horse— it shied and his jump missed; angrily he grabbed the reins and leapt on the horse, whipped it and rode away, followed by several warriors. 'That is *well*,' said Ford. 'Print it.' Mineo rode back and asked if he could try it again. Ford stared at him for a moment. 'D'ya wanna do it again with an empty camera, Sol?' Mineo grinned. 'I thought it was sloppy,' he said. 'You were very angry,' Ford explained, 'and you missed. I liked it. *Completely* in character. I don't *want* it to look perfect—like a circus.' Mineo dismounted, and started away. Ford called after

Photograph: Danny Borzage and accordion on The Wings of Eagles, *with Wayne and Bond.*

Still: Sal Mineo as Red Shirt in Cheyenne Autumn—'*I don't want it to look perfect*'.

him. 'But you can do it again with an empty camera, Sol.'

'*He knew exactly what he wanted to say,*' says director Robert Parrish, *who began as a child actor for Ford, and later worked as an editor on several of his films. 'He very seldom shot more than one take; he used very little film, and was always under schedule or under budget. So, by and large, the film that an editor would get almost* had *to go into the picture. After the shooting, he* would often go off to his boat and not come back until after the picture was cut; he did that on Young Mr Lincoln—*he had this marvellous picture and he was so sure it was right that he just took off. I think he considered all the cutters and musicians and sound effects cutters as necessary evils. On one picture—it was the last day of shooting—he said to us, "Look, the picture's finished now. I know you're going to try to louse it up—you're going to put in too much music, or over-cut it or under-cut it or something—but try not to spoil this for me because I think it's a good picture." And he went off to his boat.*'

9

Monument Valley lies within the Navajo Indian Reservation which straddles the Arizona/Utah state line. Its red buttes and mesas were caused by erosion and were named by the Indians for their shapes—the Mittens, the Big Hogan, Three Sisters—though the shadows change their appearance hour by hour. John Ford has shot all, or part, of nine movies there: *Stagecoach, My Darling Clementine, Fort Apache, She Wore A Yellow Ribbon, Wagon Master, Rio Grande, The Searchers, Sergeant Rutledge, Cheyenne Autumn.* In Hollywood they call it Ford Country; it has become so identified with him that other directors feel it would be plagiarism to make a picture there.

The location today was a stretch of sandy ground enclosed on two sides by sheer walls of red rock, a narrow canyon at one end. Wingate Smith called through his bullhorn: 'Dick Widmark, Pat Wayne, Dobe Carey, Ben Johnson! Come to the camera!' They rode up.

Ford pointed. 'When you get out there, Dick,' he said, 'you yell out, "Troop. Haaalt!" Pat, you wait till the echo dies, then you yell, "Troop. Haaalt!" ' (The second 'haaalt' was in a lower key than the first.) He put his cigar back in his mouth. Widmark and Wayne tried it once. 'O.K. Remember to wait till the echo

dies, Pat.' He turned to Johnson and Harry (Dobe) Carey, Jr. 'When Dick yells, you two advance to within six feet of him. Get the idea?' The two nodded. 'Huh?'

'Yes, sir!' they said together.

'O.K.' Ford rubbed his hands together. 'Come at a fast trot, Dick. It's fairly early on in the story—the horses are still fresh.'

After the establishing shot, Ford moved in for a closer angle on the four riders. Johnson held a red and white guidon; his horse shied. 'Let 'im be nervous,' Ford said and pushed the horse's rump. 'Now, Dick, you look up that canyon—' (he began to improvise the dialogue) '—"Plumtree!" you say. "Don't like the looks of it. Take a look up that canyon." Ben, you hold off a second.' The script supervisor was taking it down as fast as he could. 'Dick says, "Jones, you go with him." ' Ford paused. ' "Jones!" ' Another pause. ' "JONES!" ' He pointed to Carey: 'You say, "Name's *Smith,* sir." ' Back to Widmark: ' "Oh. Well, go with him!" '

Ford held his cigar from underneath and jerked his hat down further. 'When he calls out "Jones" the second time, Dobe,' he said, 'you

Still: Above the San Juan in Cheyenne Autumn.

look around behind you. You're thinkin' who the hell's Jones? Then "JONES!" Point to yourself. "Name's *Smith*, sir." Ben, take a look like ya hate like hell to ride up there—rise up in your stirrups.'

The camera rolled and Widmark called for Jones the third time. '*My* name's *Smith*, sir!' said Carey.

'"*Name's* Smith, sir!"' Ford interrupted. 'Don't try to pad your part.'

Carey nodded nervously. 'Yes, sir.' The second take: '*My* name's Smith, sir!'

'Your name's *not* Smith!' Ford yelled. 'Stop

Still: Mike Mazurki in the Victor McLaglen role, with Widmark, in Cheyenne Autumn.

tryin' to steal the scene from old Ben there.' Carey nodded again and apologized.

Third take: 'The name's Smith, sir.' There was a pause.

'Ahem,' said Ford. On the fourth take, the lines went smoothly, Johnson dug the guidon into the dirt and the two galloped off toward the canyon. 'That's *well*!' Ford called out.

'*I played music in my room every night up there on location*,' Sal Mineo says. '*Usually some*

11

kinda jazz or something—pretty loud. One night Ford comes in and asks me why I can't play that stuff a little quieter. "Well, you see, sir," I said, "this kind of music has to be played at that volume, otherwise one can't derive complete satisfaction from it." The Old Man just looked at me and took out his knife—and he opened it and laid it down on the table. "Can you play it a little softer?" he said. "Yes-sir-I-can-play-it-very-very-very-soft!" Then he picks up the knife and closes it. He nods his head, "That's what I thought," he says and goes out.'

Ford and the cast ate dinner in a small adobe building, a part of Goulding's Lodge, which is set on the lowest rim of Rock Door Mesa. There was a little dinner bell attached to the porch and it was never rung until the director had taken his place at the head of the third table from the door.

He wore a navy blue jacket tonight, khaki pants and his pajama top, the collar half up, with a shapeless sweater over it. No hat—his hair was white and whispy. He took his bone-handled jack knife out and banged it down next to him. 'I'm hawngry,' he said.

Shortly after everyone had arrived and the

food was being served, Bernard Smith (the co-producer) mentioned something about the day's shooting. 'Pat Wayne!' Ford called out.

'Sir!'

'Where's the bowl?' Wayne rose to get a little wooden bowl (filled with several dollars and quite a bit of loose change) from the piano top.

'There's a fifty-cent penalty,' Carroll Baker explained, 'for talking shop or about Mr Ford's movies at the table.'

'How much does he owe now?' said Ford.

'That last one makes two dollars, sir.' Wayne told him. The co-producer said he would pay it later.

'The other day,' said Miss Baker, 'Mr Ford was telling me something about *The Long Voyage Home*, and he stopped, paid his fifty cents and then finished the story.'

Gilbert Roland gestured for something at the far end of the table. 'Wait a minute, Luis,' Ford said (Roland's real name is Luis Antonio Alonso), 'you know you're not supposed to

Stills: The Indians ambush the Cavalry: ' A hard-nosed director who never rehearsed action'.

Stills: Homeless Indians in Cheyenne Autumn.

point. There's only three things you point at—'
Ford paused as Victor Jory passed a plate to
Roland. 'Let me get the billing right—you may
point at producers, privies, and French pastry.'

*'Ford was always a cop hater by religion, by
belief,' Parrish remembers. 'He had a big streak
of contempt for any kind of authority, any kind
of paternal influence on him—all the producers,
all the money—they were the enemy. On* The
Informer, *on the first day of shooting, he got the
entire cast and crew together in the middle of the
set, and he brought out the producer. "Now get a
good look at this guy," Ford said and he took hold
of the man's chin. "This is Cliff Reid. He is the
producer. Look at him now because you will not
see him again on this set until the picture is
finished." And that was true—we never saw him
again—he just disappeared.'*

After dinner, which had been spent playing
20 Questions (no one could guess Ford's
puzzle, which was 'Sherlock Holmes's moroc-

can slipper'), the director remained for a while,
smoking a cigar he had first cut in half with his
knife, and talking with the actors. 'Second-class
citizens,' he said, 'that's what we are.' He
drummed the palms of his hands on the table.
'In the old days, actors weren't even allowed
to be buried in Holy Ground. I mean, y'know—
"Take-your-linen-off-the-hedges, the actors
are coming to town!" '

He rose and came up behind his son, who
was still seated at the next table, and started to
inspect the top of his head. 'Who *is* this!?'
Then, with mock surprise, 'Oh!' and he started
for the door. 'I'm going to call Mother,' he said.
Pat got up and they left together.

*'I tell ya,' says Harry Goulding, who used to
own the Lodge in Monument Valley, 'to the
Navajos, Mr Ford's holy, sorta. Ev'time they've
had a rough time, boy, this thing comes outa the*

14

blue. They'd been hit pretty bad by the Depression an', by God, if an Indian'd walked into our store an' put a dollar on the counter, why Mrs Goulding an' I'd a fainted. Well, Mr Ford came here to make Stagecoach, *and gave a score a jobs to the Navajos and a lotta lives was saved. Then, just after he'd finished shootin'* She Wore A Yellow Ribbon *here, we had a blizzard that left the Valley covered with 'bout twelve feet a snow. Army planes dropped food in. Thanks to that, an' the two hundred thousand dollars or so he'd left behind, why, another tragedy was prevented. An' in '63 he heard his friends was gonna have too little t'eat, an' there he was again makin'* Cheyenne Autumn. *He's been taken into the Navajo tribe, you know. They have a special name for 'im, the Navajos. Natani Nez. That's his name, only his. Natani Nez. It means the Tall Soldier.'*

Twenty-five miles from the Lodge flows the San Juan River. Red cliffs rise high above it,

and down at the bank are small trees and weeds and piles of silver driftwood. The water is the colour of clay.

Playing the Cheyenne, Navajo men and women on horseback and pulling travois were assembled at the river's edge; among them were several stuntmen dressed and made-up as Indians. On the cliff above, and several hundred yards back from the edge, was the Cavalry. Lee and Frank Bradley, Navajo interpreters who had worked on eleven other Ford films, were shouting instructions to the Indians through bullhorns. Wingate Smith was yelling orders.

Ford collared one of the wranglers. 'Can Carroll go in the river with the wagon?'

'Well, where I went in—'

'Don't give me the story of your life,' Ford threw his cigar away, 'just answer the question.'

The man said that she could.

Ford nodded sharply. 'Good.' He pulled a

long white handkerchief from his back pocket. Beetson was there to hand him a bullhorn; he spoke through it. 'Okay, Lee. Frank. Start your people across.' He chewed on one corner of the handkerchief, the bulk of which hung down over his chest. 'Easy!' The interpreters relayed the instructions and slowly the Navajos moved into the water. Ford called to Chuck Hayward (stuntman), who was halfway across the river. 'All right, hold 'em there, Chuck! That's *well*!' The Navajos were spread out through the water, holding in place. 'Fill up those empty spaces and get those travois up there!' Then Ford gave some instructions to the Cavalry, at which the camera was pointed.

'Okay, we're rolling,' said Ford.

'Speed,' said the camera operator, Eddie Garvin.

'All right. *Dick*!' The Cavalry rode forward at a steady clip. 'All right. Lee! Frank! Start 'em moving!' The tribe moved slowly through the water below. Widmark raised his arm. 'Troooop. Haaalt!' Pat Wayne echoed him (in a slightly lower register). The Cavalry stopped and Widmark looked downwards at the Indians. The camera slowly followed his look; it panned from the troops across the barren, rocky slopes, down and around to the Navajos; some had

reached the other side, others were still moving across the gray river, their horses leaping up and down. The only sounds were of horses whinnying and of the movement of bodies through water. 'That is *well*! Now get those people outa there—dry 'em off—get 'em some coffee or something—'

'*I was very careful,*' says Stewart, '*I really watched my step on* The Man Who Shot Liberty Valance. *Besides, he was givin' it to Duke Wayne all the time. And we were in the last two weeks of shooting and hardly a murmur. Then one day we're shooting the funeral scene . . . coffin there,* and Woody Strode was in his old-age makeup,' Stewart says, referring to the Negro actor who has been in several Ford films. 'He had coveralls on and a hat. Ford came over to me, he nodded at Woody. "What d'ya think of Woody's costume?" I paused and then I said, "Waall, s'a little Uncle Remus, isn't it?" Now . . . nooow why . . . why I . . . I wished I could've just taken those words and just . . . just . . .' Stewart's hand is under his chin and with his trembling fingers he gestures putting the words back until finally all his fingers are in his mouth. 'He just looked at me . . . just looked and I knew what was . . . I knew . . . He says, "And what's wrong with Uncle Remus?" I said, "Why, nothing." He says, "I put that costume together—that's just what I intended!" "Listen, Boss," I said—"Woody, Duke, everybody, c'mon over here." An' everybody comes over. "Look at Woody," he says. "Look at his* costume," *he says. "Looks like Uncle* Remus, *doesn't it?" "Yes, Boss, yes, Coach, yes, sir,' they said—like a bunch a parrots. "One of the* players," *he goes on. "One of the players seems to have some objection! One of the players here doesn't seem to like Uncle Remus! As a matter of fact, I'm not at all sure he even likes* Negroes!"' *Stewart shakes his head. 'Wayne said to me later, "Ya thought ya were gonna make it through all right, didn't you?"'*

A group of twenty or thirty Cheyenne war-

riors were to come over a sandy hill, charging down toward the Cavalry and the camera. Ford attended to the stuntmen's costumes individually and gave instructions to Hayward, who was to lead the ambush. Two men from *Life* Magazine, a photographer and a writer, were visiting the set.

After half an hour of preparation, Ford sat next to the camera, crossed his legs and lifted the bullhorn. The camera was trained on the top of the hill where nothing was visible yet. 'Okay. We're rolling,' he said.

'Speed!' said Garvin.

Stills: Cheyenne Autumn; *left— Carroll Baker with Nanomba 'Moonbeam' Morton.*

'All right, Chuck!' Ford called through the bullhorn, and a score of horsemen came galloping over the hill, whooping and firing their rifles; the Cavalry at the bottom fired back. The shots reverberated loudly in the valley as the riders swooped down the hill, dust flying, and thundered by the camera so closely that Ford's bullhorn was knocked from his hand. He did not move. An Indian had fallen off his horse and lay midway down the hill. The camera

17

panned the Indians off into the distance. 'That's *well!*'

Several people ran out to see if the Navajo was hurt, but he was walking gingerly away before they got to him. Another group clustered near Ford, and one man, displaying the crushed bullhorn, shook his head. 'We damn near went home early today,' he said. Nearby, another technician was pointing out how close the horse's hooves had come to hitting Ford. 'It wouldn't dare,' said his partner.

The director had got up from his chair, and he turned to the company. 'Tomorrow we'll do it with film,' he announced. 'That was for *Life Magazine!*'

'*I told Mr. Ford I wanted to wear my hair down for* Cheyenne Autumn,' *says Miss Baker. 'Like the women in Ingmar Bergman's films. He said, "Ingrid Bergman?" "No," I said. "Ingmar Bergman." "Who's he?" I said, "Bergman, you know, the great Swedish director." He let it go and I saw fit to change the subject. But as I was leaving, he said, "Oh, Ingmar Bergman—you mean the fella that called me the greatest director in the world."* '

'Goddamn that hoss *did* hit me,' Ford said at lunch, and rolled up one trouser leg; there was a bruise. He turned to the *Life* reporter. 'In your story—you say it was broken.' The waitress who served the lunches on location asked him if he wanted another cup of coffee. 'I'm sick and tired of answering questions!' he said loudly. The girl moved away quickly. 'Pat!' Ford called her. She turned. 'Could I please have a cup of coffee? Since you're up . . .' She laughed and went to get it for him. He turned to Miss Baker. 'Carroll, you wanna look at my leg?' He lifted the trouser leg again. 'They told me I should get somebody to take a look at it.' He turned to Dolores Del Rio. 'Dolores, *you* wanna look at my leg?'

Later, Ford was telling the others about the Navajo medicine man. 'The original one was a fella named Fat—this fella we have now is just one of his disciples. I used to tell Harry Goulding and get anything I ordered. Thunderclouds . . . One night I said to Harry, "Tell 'im we need snow. Need the Valley covered with snow." Next morning, I stepped outa my room. A thin layer of snow covered the Valley.' A Navajo with a lined face and hair braided with red cloth came up. 'This is the *new* medicine man.' 'Yat'hey', he said to the Navajo.

'Yat'hey.'

Ford raised his arm and waved at the sky. 'Nijone.' He nodded his head and the man smiled. 'Ah'sheh'eh,' Ford waved again. 'Nijone.' The Navajo nodded, and moved away. 'There's no word for fleecy clouds in Navajo, so it's a little difficult. The first time he did it, he got 'em just right.' He paused. 'But they were in the wrong place!'

'*I was President of the Directors Guild in the 50's,' says Joseph L. Mankiewicz, 'during the*

McCarthy Era, and a faction of the Guild, headed by DeMille, tried to make it mandatory for every member to sign a loyalty oath. I was in Europe when the thing started, but as soon as they notified me, I sent word that, as President, I was very much against anything like that. Well, pretty soon, these little items about me started appearing in the gossip columns. "Isn't it a pity about Joe Mankiewicz? We didn't know he was a pinko." In those days, you know, an insinuation was almost as good as a proven fact. Well, it really got serious—I began to realize my career was on the block. They called a meeting of the entire Guild, finally, and I flew back for it. The entire membership showed up. It was harrowing— DeMille's group made speeches—four hours it went on. And all during this, I was wondering, and I knew quite a few others were wondering, what John Ford thought. He was kind of the Grand Old Man of the Guild and people could be influenced by him. But he just sat there on the aisle wearing his baseball cap and sneakers, didn't say a word. Then after DeMille had made his big speech, there was silence for a moment and Ford raised his hand. We had a court stenographer there to take it all down and everybody had to identify themselves for the record. So Ford stood up. "My name's John Ford," he said. "I make Westerns." He praised DeMille's pictures and DeMille as a director. "I don't think there's anyone in this room," he said, "who knows more about what the American public wants than Cecil B. DeMille—and he certainly knows how to give it to them." Then he looked right at DeMille, who was across the hall from him. "But I don't like you, C. B.," he said. "And I don't like what you've been saying here tonight. Now I move we give Joe a vote of confidence—and let's all go home and get some sleep." And that's what they did.'

Pat Ford came by on horseback, a pipe in his mouth, his hat pulled down front and back. There had been a rumour that *Cheyenne Autumn*

would be his father's farewell to the Western. 'Hell! Why, he'll be makin' Westerns a couple a years after he's dead.' Pat kicked his horse and it started forward; he took the pipe from his mouth. 'He loves these cowboys and Indians and this valley.' He rode off to join the Cavalry.

Stills: Winter in Cheyenne Autumn—*the Cavalry (left) and Ricardo Montalban and Gilbert Roland (below) as Little Wolf and Dull Knife.*

19

2 POET AND COMEDIAN

At one point in our interview, Mr Ford was talking about a cut sequence from *Young Mr Lincoln*, and he described Lincoln as a shabby figure, riding into town on a mule, stopping to gaze at a theatre poster. 'This poor ape,' he said, 'wishing he had enough money to see "Hamlet".' Reading over the edited version of the interview, it was one of the few things Ford asked me to change; he said he didn't much like 'the idea of calling Mr Lincoln a poor ape.' Seeing it in print, one might understand his reservation—but when he said it, there was such an extraordinary sense of intimacy in his tone (and as much affection as there was in a reference to John Wayne as 'this big oaf'), that somehow it was no longer a director speaking of a great President, but a man talking about a friend.

'Spig' Wead and Johnny Buckley were close friends in Ford's life, yet his films about them (*The Wings of Eagles* and *They Were Expendable*) are no more personal than his picture of Lincoln. In fact, this is the very thing that makes *Young Mr Lincoln* such a great movie: Ford's *rapport* with Lincoln brings him to life, makes us understand and admire the *man*—not some remote figure in history whom we are supposed to revere.

It is part of Ford's genius that he can also convey the man's larger significance. At the end of the film, Lincoln walks up a hill alone in the midst of a thunderstorm—a simple poetic vision of the young man's destiny. What makes it so moving (apart from its beauty) is that we *know* what the image means, but this person we have come to care about does not.

Lincoln appears briefly in *The Prisoner of Shark Island* (made before the other film), and again Ford is able to present the man on two levels. The Civil War has just ended and a band has come to play for the President; what song would he like to hear? He asks them to play 'Dixie'. (As an example of the inter-relationships in Ford's work, we have the scene in *Young Mr Lincoln*, wherein he unknowingly plays 'Dixie', calling it a 'catchy' tune.) Shortly afterwards, he is assassinated, and Ford creates a memorable image: the haunting shot of Lincoln's head slumped to the side seems to become a still frame, and a thin curtain, like the veil of history, is drawn over it. As Andrew Sarris has said, Ford's work is 'a double vision of an event in all its vital immediacy and also

Still: Cheyenne Autumn—*Carl Schurz (Edward G. Robinson) and his 'old friend'.*

20

in its ultimate memory-image on the horizon of history.' (*Film Culture*, No. 28, Spring 1963.)

Asked which American directors most appeal to him, Orson Welles answered, '. . . the old masters. By which I mean John Ford, John Ford and John Ford . . . With Ford at his best, you feel that the movie has lived and breathed in a real world . . .' (*Playboy*, March 1967). It would be instructive (in fact schools might do well making it a regular course) to run Ford's films about the United States in historical chronology—because he has told the American saga in human terms and made it come alive.

Still: Henry Fonda as Young Mr Lincoln.

Sarris again: 'No American director has ranged so far across the landscape of the American past, the worlds of Lincoln, Lee, Twain, O'Neill, the three great wars, the Western and trans-Atlantic migrations, the horseless Indians of the Mohawk Valley and the Sioux and Comanche cavalries of the West, the Irish and Spanish incursions, and the delicately balanced politics of polyglot cities and border states.' (*Film Culture*, No. 25, Summer 1962). What Ford can do better than any film-maker in the world is create an epic canvas and still people it with characters of equal size and importance —no matter how lowly they may be.

It is not the concentration on Americana, however, that gives his work its unity, but the singular poetic vision with which he sees all life. His most frequently recurring theme is defeat, failure: the tragedy of it, but also the peculiar glory inherent in it. It is significant that the first film he made after his experience of World War II (*They Were Expendable*) should centre around one of America's worst defeats—the Philippines. Since his last film before the war (*How Green Was My Valley*) told of the disintegration of a family and an entire way of life (which, in essence, is also the theme of *Mother Machree, Four Sons, The Grapes of Wrath*, even *Tobacco Road* as he told it), one cannot say that his post-war work was a reaction to what he had seen abroad—though it is true that through the late forties, the fifties and sixties his films became increasingly melancholy. (And better. Too many critics neatly

Still: the family of How Green Was My Valley: *Crisp (left), McDowall, Anna Lee.*

categorize his thirties pictures, *The Informer* and *Stagecoach*, as his best, while any one of a score of later films is superior, not only in execution but in depth of expression.)

Fort Apache, then, is the story of a last stand, just as *She Wore A Yellow Ribbon* tells of an aging soldier's final mission before an enforced retirement. The heroes of *The Long Gray Line* and *The Wings of Eagles* never succeeded in the ways they had wanted to. The old Mayor's campaign for re-election in *The Last Hurrah* ends in defeat and death. Even *My Darling Clementine*, in which Wyatt Earp has been triumphant, ends with the reminder that a man has lost two of his three brothers. *The Man Who Shot Liberty Valance* is as much the story of one person's sacrifice for another as *7 Women* is, and both are tinged with an aching bitterness. (Sacrifice as a variation of Ford's central theme can be found in many of his films, among them, *The Outcasts of Poker Flat*, *Marked Men* and its remake, *Three Godfathers*, *The Wallop*, *Desperate Trails*, *Hearts of Oak*, *3 Bad Men*, *Men Without Women*.)

At the end of *Hangman's House* (1928), Citizen Hogan (Victor McLaglen), an exiled Irish patriot who has risked his life by returning to Ireland and helping a young couple, must nevertheless leave his country again; he is still an outlaw there. The boy he has helped thanks him and the girl gives him a kiss; they walk off into the night mist, but the camera lingers on Hogan. He is looking after them, and for the first time in the film we realize that he loves the girl; he loves Ireland too, and must leave them both now—probably forever. The film ends on that shot of McLaglen gazing wistfully into the dark, anticipating the final moment of *The Searchers*—made almost thirty years later—in which Ethan (John Wayne), who has spent ten years of his life searching for a little girl kidnapped by Indians, walks slowly away from her family's home—where he is always welcome but where he will always be an outsider—as the door slowly closes on him.

I was fortunate to see a dozen of Ford's early Fox films (1920–1935) and, though most of them were assignments, there was in even the least of them something thoroughly his: from an evocative, fleeting image of a city street reflected in a shop window (in *Riley the Cop*) to several shots in *Lightnin'* that have about them the same sense of futility that was to distinguish the look of *Tobacco Road*; from the horse race in *Hangman's House* which forecasts (and betters) the one in *The Quiet Man* (there is also an underground meeting place in the film identical to one in *The Informer*), to a moment in *Pilgrimage* as beautiful as any he has done: a mother, having heard of her son's death in the war, sits at her desk, expressionless, piecing together a photograph of the boy she had once torn in anger. There is the boastful, blustering Irishman in *Seas Beneath*—whom McLaglen was later to personify in a half-dozen films—and, through them all, the photography.

In *Just Pals* (1920), though Griffith's influence is apparent, Ford has already developed his own signature (without the sometimes flowery Griffith flourishes). The plot may be filled with devices and melodrama, but here is the same naturalness in the playing, the same understanding of simple people and attention to detail that was to distinguish his later work; here is Ford's Montana town, with its picket fences and distant camp fires, the back-lit clouds of dust, the unerring eye for composition, and the same dynamic sense of the movies' narrative power.

This last was most apparent in the magnificent landrush sequence in *3 Bad Men* (1926), a film unjustly overshadowed by *The Iron Horse*, which he had made two years earlier

Still: The Wings of Eagles—*the story of a close friend: John Wayne as 'Spig' Wead.*

Photograph: Ford (kneeling by camera) on The Iron Horse—*his first international success.*

and which was more successful critically. The later picture, however, is better in many ways and more personal to Ford. Here (in embryo form) are several of his trademarks: the fancy-dressed sheriff, the drunken newspaper editor, the good bad men (who sacrifice themselves in the end), and, as always, the Fordian images of riders on the horizon, striking long shots of wagons and men, vivid contrasts of darkness and light.

The great problem in studying Ford is that over half his work cannot be seen. By the time he made *The Iron Horse* (the earliest of his

films at least partially available), he had already directed over thirty-five features (plus almost a dozen two-reelers). More than most directors can do in a lifetime (especially today), he had accomplished in less than eight years. Many of these pictures may have been primitive in story and characters, but all reports of the time (see filmography) indicate they were visually distinctive from the beginning. (His first feature, *Straight Shooting*, made in 1917, turned up at

the Montreal Festival two years ago, and impressed those who saw it with its unmistakably Fordian look.) Although plot synopses are always deceptive (in favour of a picture sometimes, but more often against it), a look at the early stories leads one to believe that several films would be of considerably more than just historical interest. *Hell Bent, Riders of Vengeance, The Outcasts of Poker Flat, Marked Men, Desperate Trails*—these and at least a dozen others must be seen before any real evaluation can be made of Ford's early work.

However, it is possible to surmise (still based

Still: Earle Foxe (centre) in Upstream (*1927*), *one of Ford's many Fox assignments.*

on the stories) that his Universal period (1917–1921) was more interesting and personal than his work at Fox during the remainder of the silent era. During those first five years with Harry Carey, he was able to write his own scripts, and, although almost all the pictures were westerns, he had considerable freedom within the form. At Fox, however, he was handed a great many assignments for which he admits having had little or no affection (though,

27

as he also says, he *enjoys* making pictures, often despite the scenarios). Rarely did he have the opportunity to do projects of his own choosing, and it is interesting that when he did they were not only his best films (which one would expect), but also his most successful: *The Iron Horse, 3 Bad Men, Four Sons.*

Certainly the Fox period had more value to his career than his days at Universal. Quite apart from what it may have done for his work —broadening his scale, perhaps, and his scope —it increased his power in the industry, which is not unimportant in an art ruled by box office.

(And one should remember that Ford remains not only the most honoured American film-maker—with six Academy Awards and four New York Film Critics' Awards—but also a director whose work has consistently made money for the studios which financed it.) He knows, however, that in Hollywood you don't win prestige or prizes making westerns. As he once told a reporter: 'Every time I start to make a western, they say, "There goes senile old John Ford out West again".' (*Cosmopolitan*, March 1964).

Clearly, it has plagued him all his life, and

28

Stills: Ford's calculated artistry. Left— The
Informer. *Above*— The Fugitive.

it is significant that not one of his Oscars —and
only one Critics' Award—was for a western.
'They have kept the industry going,' Ford has
said, but he knows that the industry also looks
down on them. Nonetheless, one feels that the
least of his Harry Carey westerns would have
more interest today than such higher budgeted
Fox specials as *Kentucky Pride* (banal, though
not unappealing), *Hoodman Blind*, *Thank You*,
Upstream, or *The Face on the Barroom Floor*.

With the coming of sound (and his first films
away from Fox since 1921), Ford's career
alternated between projects he wanted to do
(*Salute, Men Without Women, Up the River,
Arrowsmith*) and assignments (*Born Reckless,
The Brat, The World Moves On*). But the key
to his work in the thirties lies in a personal
struggle (no doubt unconscious) between two
very different kinds of film, both of which
interested him deeply: the dramas, like *The
Lost Patrol* or *The Informer*, and the lighter
pictures of American life, such as the Will
Rogers trilogy (1933–35). Critics, of course,

29

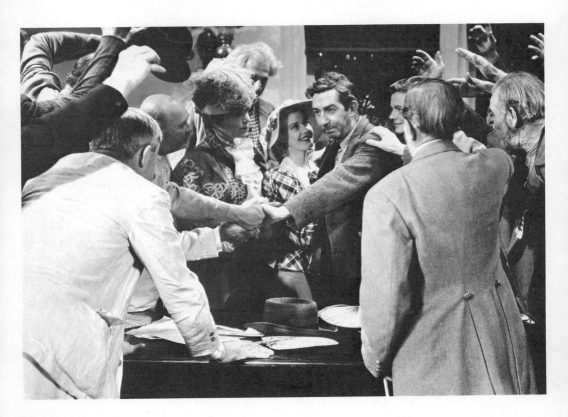

were far more impressed with the calculated artistry of *The Informer* than with the artlessness of *Judge Priest* or *Steamboat Round the Bend*, but as Ford's career has evolved into the 'fifties and 'sixties, it has become increasingly clear that the latter films are closer to his real character, and, essentially, deeper works of art.

This intriguing duality continued into the forties, during which Ford would make a very consciously artistic *The Long Voyage Home* one year, and a far less studied (and more emotional) *How Green Was My Valley* the next. The stirring imagery of his cavalry trilogy (1948–50)

Stills: Will Rogers (above, at left) as Judge Priest; *Charles Winninger in the same role, with Russell Simpson, in* The Sun Shines Bright.

seems to have more of his heart in it than the exquisite pictorialism of *The Fugitive* (1947). In fact, the bold, vigorous strokes of *The Searchers*, or the seeming simplicity of *Wagon Master* require more artistry than the direction of *The Informer*—a film that Ford feels today 'lacks humour—which is my forte'.

And Welles has said, 'John Ford is a poet.

A comedian.' (*Cahiers du Cinéma* 165.) In Ford's best films, these two sides of his personality are mixed: it is, after all, the mingling of comedy and pathos in *The Sun Shines Bright* (an informal remake of the Will Rogers picture, *Judge Priest*) that gives the film its remarkable sense of humanity, just as the abrupt switches from comedy to tragedy in *The Wings of Eagles* give it such an extraordinary feeling of truth.

Every Ford movie is filled with reverberations from another—which makes his use of the same players from year to year, decade to decade, so much more than just building 'a stock company'—and one film of his cannot really be looked at as separate from the rest. What Ma Joad says of her life (in *The Grapes of Wrath*) is true also of Ford's work: '. . . it's all one flow, like a stream, little eddies, little waterfalls, but the river it goes right on.' Ranse and Hallie Stoddard (James Stewart and Vera Miles) return to Shinbone for the funeral of Tom Doniphon (John Wayne) at the start of *The Man Who Shot Liberty Valance*, and Hallie visits the ruins of Doniphon's ranchhouse, where she picks a cactus rose, a wild flower symbolizing Doniphon's Old West, which is as dead as he is. A haunting musical theme is heard during this scene, and when one realizes it is the same music Ford used after the death of Ann Rutledge in *Young Mr Lincoln*, its meaning in *Liberty Valance* is heightened. For Ann Rutledge was the lost love of Lincoln's youth, just as Tom Doniphon is Hallie's.

Ask Ford about this, and he'll tell you he just used the tune because it's among his favourites, that's all. But one can't help wondering, if he likes it so much, why he waited twenty-three years to use it again, unless—

whether consciously or not—he felt at last that it *fitted*. And herein lies a personal duality in Ford, the artist. He seems to operate on instinct. (Certainly the making of a film is second-nature to him—he never plans a sequence out on paper, knowing exactly how each shot will cut with the next, and, at a glance, where his camera should be.) This is an image of himself he likes to encourage. Though he genuinely does not like to be interviewed and becomes

Photograph: Ford directing Stagecoach, *his first sound western—' really " Boule-de-suif ".'*

Still: Henry Fonda as Young Mr Lincoln, with Pauline Moore as Ann Rutledge

bored discussing his films, he will go out of his way to discourage the conception that he is a man who consciously tries to create something of value or that his work has any continuity whatever. If Ford can convince you that he's 'a hard-nosed director' who just takes a script and does it, he is content.

But the truth, I think, lies elsewhere. Welles' description is profound: 'A poet. A comedian.' Both facets of the Ford personality are instinctual, but 'comedian' implies a certain conscious showmanship and this is very clear in his work. He is neither unaware of his effects nor are any of them unintentional. But—like poets and comedians—he neither likes to explain a joke nor theorize about a ballad. He simply creates them.

33

Ford's work, like his personality, is filled with ambiguities. 'When the legend becomes fact,' says a newspaper editor near the end of *Liberty Valance*, 'print the legend.' And this in a film that has just *exposed* a legend: Stoddard, famous as 'the man who shot Liberty Valance', has finally told the truth: it was Doniphon who actually killed the notorious outlaw. 'Print the legend.' Ford prints the fact. In *Fort Apache*, Col Thursday (Henry Fonda) underestimates his Indian opponent and arrogantly leads his men into a massacre. But, at the end, the newspapers—with the help of those Army men who witnessed the spectacle—are writing the birth of a legend, creating a noble leader who died with his men. Yet Ford has just shown us the facts: Thursday was wrong; his men died in vain. On the other hand—and here is a further level of meaning—Ford is saying that the Cavalry, in fact the country, lives on despite the errors of any one leader; and if printing a falsehood will help the morale of the Cavalry or the nation—then print the legend.

But Ford, never dogmatic, has also shown us the truth—just as his Catholicism does not stop him from making *7 Women*, in which the heroine is an agnostic who gives up her life for a group of Christian missionaries, the leader of whom is a far from appealing religious fanatic. But then Ford's sympathies have always been with the outsider, the dispossessed. The homeless Indians of *Cheyenne Autumn* are not far removed from the wandering Oakies of *The Grapes of Wrath*.

In his desire not to be typed 'a Western director' (it is revealing that he waited ten years before making his first sound western, *Stagecoach*), Ford has been versatile through his career, and many of his finest pictures are far removed from that genre: *They Were Expendable*, *The Quiet Man*, *The Long Gray Line*, *The Wings of Eagles*, *The Last Hurrah*. Yet he has made more of them than anything else, and his

personality is most clearly reflected in his westerns: to follow their mood since 1950, for example, is to see a key progression. Having reached the height of optimism in *Wagon Master*, that most inspiring story of pioneer spirit, Ford completed his cavalry trilogy (in the same year) with *Rio Grande*, a film that mingled feelings of loss (the Civil War—the burning of the Shenandoah Valley) with the glorified charges of the Apache wars. His next western, made six years later, showed the beginning of a change: an epic story, filled with comedy and drama, *The Searchers* nonetheless ends on a tragic note as the man of the West goes off alone. *The Horse Soldiers*, *Sergeant Rutledge* and *Two Rode Together* are increasingly bitter in spirit, until with *The Man Who Shot Liberty Valance* (his most important film of the sixties), he seems to be making his final statement on the western. (The subsequent 'Wild West' interlude in *Cheyenne Autumn* is treated as farce—the Wyatt Earp he glorified in *My Darling Clementine* has become a wily joker.) Doniphon, the epitome of the Old West, dies without his boots on, without his gun, and receives a pauper's funeral, but the man of the New West, the man of books, has ridden to success on the achievements of the first, who was discarded, forgotten. It is perhaps the most mournful, tragic film Ford has made. There is nothing wrong with the New West—it was inevitable; yet as they ride back East, Stoddard and Hallie look out of their train window at the passing western landscape and Hallie comments on how untamed it used to be, and how it has changed, almost into a garden. But one feels that Ford's love, like Hallie's, remains with the wildness of the cactus rose.

Still: The Man Who Shot Liberty Valance—*Tom Doniphon gives Hallie a cactus rose*—*Stewart, Strode, Vera Miles, Wayne, Qualen, Jeanette Nolan.*

3 A JOB OF WORK

[The following is an edited version of an interview with Mr Ford tape recorded at his home in Bel Air, California, over a period of seven days in the Summer and Fall of 1966.]

Did your parents meet in Ireland?

No, they lived in the same village and never met there. Of course a village encompasses quite a bit of ground—the post office is the village and there might be a few houses and a pub—but the hills would be part of the village too, and my father lived at one end of this area and my mother at the other. They might have seen one another in church, but they met in America.

My father came over first—to get into the Civil War. He was only fifteen but he was a huge man, and he already had four brothers in the war—one on the Confederate side who was killed, two on the Union side, and one who was on both sides—he got *two* pensions. But by the time my father arrived, the war was over. I asked him, 'Which side was you going to fight for, Daddo?' He said, 'Oh, it didn't make no difference—either side.'

Why did you and your brother Francis take the name Ford?

After having worked around in stock com-

panies, my brother went to New York and became stage manager for some company that was going to do a Broadway show; having a very retentive memory, he also understudied four or five parts. The night of the opening, the fellow who was playing one of the important roles—a comedy part—got drunk or broke his leg or something—I think the former. So my brother Frank stepped into the part and made a hit of it. But the name on the bill was 'Ford'— so from then on that was his name—he could never get rid of it; neither could I—I was always called Ford. A few years later, a fellow came up to me and said, 'I'd like to have a job —I'm a pretty good actor.' I said, 'You're a good type—what's your name?' He said, 'Frank Feeney.' I said, 'That's very funny—that's my brother's real name.' He said, 'I know—I'm the original Francis Ford—the one that got dru—I mean, broke his leg the night your brother took the part!' I thought it was such a funny gag, I gave him a good part. He changed his name to something else and worked for years. I think he's passed away now.

Is it true that you played the leading role in several two-reelers?

I played the lead in a picture!? With my looks? Good God! Well, I know I did a lot of stunts—

catching the speeding train on horseback, jumping a horse off the cliff, that sort of thing. I used to do most of my brother's stunts—we looked alike and were built alike. Got about $15 a week.

How did you first get a chance to direct?

Well, I was quite young at the time. I had worked as a labourer, prop man, assistant director. Then, when Carl Laemmle visited the Universal Studios from New York for the first

Photograph: Ford (seated, right) shooting the bee sequence for Lightnin' *(1925).*

time, they gave him a big party on the only closed stage on the lot. I was a prop boy then and doubled as a bartender. The party lasted most of the night, and I slept under the bar so I could be on time for work in the morning. But when I reported, neither the director nor any of the actors were there—they'd been up all night. Some of the cowboy extras were there and nobody else. Isadore Bernstein, who was the General Manager then and a very wonderful person, got very upset when he saw the situation. 'The Boss is coming,' he said. 'We've got to *do* something.' I said, 'What?' 'Any-

thing,' he said. So when Mr Laemmle and his party came, I told the cowboys to go down to the end of the street and ride back toward the camera fast, yelling like hell. Laemmle seemed to like that, so Mr Bernstein said, 'Try and do something else.' 'Well,' I said, 'all I can do is have 'em ride back.' He says, 'Well, do that.' So I told the cowboys, 'When I fire a shot, I want several of you guys to fall off your horses.' Now there were a lot of pretty girls in Mr Laemmle's party, so when I fired a shot, every damn cowboy fell off his horse—showing off, you see. 'Can't you do something else?' said

Still: Harry Carey, with Neva Gerber (centre) and Mrs. Townsend in Three Mounted Men (*1918*).

Bernstein. So we burned the street down. They came riding back and forth—it was more like a pogrom than a Western. Months later, Mr Laemmle said, 'Give Jack Ford the job—he yells good.'

Well, they needed somebody to direct a cheap picture of no consequence with Harry Carey, whose contract was running out. I knew Harry very well and admired him; I told him this idea I had and he said, 'That's good, let's do it.' I said, 'Well, we haven't a typewriter,' and he said, 'Oh, hell, we don't need that, we can make it up as we go along.' So we went out and made it, and it turned out to be their best picture that year.

We kept on making pictures even after Harry's contract ran out, until finally he and his wife, Ollie, went back to New York for a visit. It seems everyone in the company office was very friendly and pretty soon Ollie found out that Harry was the leading star of Universal! And his contract had run out. Well, he'd been getting $75 a week—now he signed up again at $1,250. I'd been getting $50 a week as an assistant director, but when I started directing it went down to $35—don't ask me why; when Harry signed his new contract, I started getting $75 a week—which was big dough in those days.

What were the early westerns with Carey like?
They weren't shoot-'em-ups, they were character stories. Carey was a great actor, and we didn't dress him up like the cowboys you see on TV—all dolled up. There were numerous Western stars around that time—Mix and Hart and Buck Jones—and they had several actors at Universal whom they were grooming to be Western leading men; now we knew we were going to be through anyway in a couple of weeks, and so we decided to kid them a little bit—not kid the Western—but the leading men —and make Carey sort of a bum, a saddle tramp, instead of a great bold gun-fighting hero. All this was fifty percent Carey and fifty percent me. He always wore a dirty blue shirt and an old vest, patched overalls, very seldom carried a gun—and he didn't own a hat. On each picture, the cowboys would line up and he'd go down the line and finally pick one of their hats and wear that; it would please the owner because it meant he worked all through that picture. I used to say to Harry, 'Why don't you go downtown, spend some dough and buy a

Still: Harry Carey as ' honest gambler ' John Oakhurst in The Outcasts of Poker Flat (*1919*).

hat?' He'd say, 'Oh, hell, there are millions of 'em around here—I can always borrow one.' He became one of the big stars.

If we had a gunfight, we'd talk it over with someone who'd been an old lawman—like Pardner Jones—and he'd tell us how it would have happened. In those days we didn't have any tricks—if you had to have a glass shot out of somebody's hand, Pardner would actually shoot it out—with a rifle. (It's hanging up downstairs—he left it to me.) **Pardner was the one who rode the wild horse in front of Queen Victoria when the Buffalo Bill Show went to London;** this was a horse that couldn't be ridden and Pardner rode it. He was also the lawman who killed the Apache Kid. He used to tell us that none of those fellows—Wild Bill Hickok, Wyatt Earp—had been great shots with a pistol. 'I'm not a great shot with a pistol,' Pardner said, 'I never knew one. The idea was to over-awe the man, get as close as you could. If you had a *real* fight on your hands, you used a rifle.' Pardner used to say, 'If a man reached to draw a gun from his holster, he'd be dead before he got it out.' Just for an experiment, we put up a target at twenty-five paces, and we all started shooting at it with Colt '45s. None of us hit it. (We all used to *pull* the trigger until one of the lawmen walked through and told us to *squeeze* it.) Pardner couldn't hit the ceiling with a pistol, but then he'd take a rifle and put a *dime* up there twenty-five yards away and hit it. So we tried to do it the real way it had been in the West: none of this so-called quick-draw stuff, nobody wore flashy clothes and we didn't have dance hall scenes with the girls in short dresses. As Pardner said, 'In Tombstone, we never saw anything like that.'

Did you also deglamorize Tom Mix and Hoot Gibson when you worked with them later?
Well, Tom had an image—he was the well-dressed cowboy—and that's all he could do. I toned him down a little bit. But we did the same thing with Hoot as we did with Harry. Only Hoot had a hat.

How did you make the films in those early days?
Well, with Carey, he and I usually wrote our own scripts. We finally got a writer who'd take it down in shorthand and tap it out for the crew—so they would have some idea of what we were doing—because we certainly didn't know. The two-reelers were made in about five days, six at the most. We all used to ride our horses out to the location; we'd shoot till it got dark and then we'd camp out in sleeping bags. We just stayed there till we'd finished the picture and then we rode back. We used to run our rushes in the negative in those days, so you couldn't tell a damn thing about them.

Who were your early influences?
Well, my brother Frank. He was a great cameraman—there's nothing they're doing today—all these things that are supposed to be so new—that he hadn't done; he was really a good artist, a wonderful musician, a hell of a good actor, a good director—Johnny of all trades—and *master* of all; he just couldn't concentrate on one thing too long. But he was the only influence *I* ever had, working in pictures. I certainly had no desire to go into pictures or have anything to do with them. Still haven't.

How did it happen then?
Hungry.

Do you feel you were influenced by Griffith in the early films?
Oh, D. W. Griffith influenced all of us. If it weren't for Griffith, we'd probably still be in the infantile phase of motion pictures. He started it all—he invented the close-up and a lot of things nobody had thought of doing before. Griffith was the one who made it an art—if you can call it an art—but at least he made it something worthwhile.

Did you know him well?
I knew him—not intimately. I was a great admirer of his and just a kid at the time, but he was very friendly with me; you know, he'd pat me on the shoulder, and once when I got fired from Universal as a second assistant prop man, I rode with the Klansmen in *The Birth of A Nation*. I was the one with the glasses. I was riding with one hand holding the hood up so I could see because the damn thing kept slipping

Still: Ford's original Three Godfathers—Harry Carey, Winifred Westover in Marked Men.

40

over my glasses. But we were quite friendly, and as he got older, we became more friendly.

Do you remember any of your early films with particular fondness?

Well, it's a long time ago and to me, you make a picture and that's it—go on to something else, forget about it. But I can remember some funny things that happened. For example, there was a fellow named Mario Caracciolo, called himself Mario Carillo—he came over here with Valentino; he'd been a captain in the Italian Army, but he wanted to be an actor. Valentino became famous and got rid of him right away, so Mario used to work with me a lot, playing bits. I'd have him do gamblers—he was so handsome, you know, all dressed up, dealing the cards. On one picture, he was the leader of a posse chasing Carey. We were out on location and it was a very tough ride, so we got the stuntmen ready to do the shot. Mario came over

Photograph: The recurring figure of Lincoln—Ford directs Judge Bull in The Iron Horse.

to me and he said, 'I am lousy.' I said, 'No. What's the matter?' He says, 'I stink.' 'No, Mario—why? What's the matter?' He points at the stuntman who was dressed up like him. 'Then who is that man playing my part?' I said, 'Oh, that's your double.' 'Double?' he says. 'Yes, he's going to ride for you.' 'He's gonna ride for me?' I said, 'Yes.' 'Why?' 'Well,' I said, 'he's a cowboy, he's used to this.' 'Ohhh,' he says, 'he rides for *me*—that's *me*.' I said, 'Yes.' Well, anyway, we got the shot ready and when I said 'Action,' my God, out dashed *two* gamblers! Well, one of them was superb—he hit that

hill and slid his horse down, rode up the next hill and slid the horse down—it was Mario. He left the others far behind. Turned out he was the leader of a famous Italian riding team. Of course, we couldn't use the shot, but we did it again and let him do his own riding.

Now, years later, my family and I were taking a trip to Italy, and as we were coming into Gibraltar an announcement was made that lunch would be three quarters of an hour late, because His Excellency, the Italian Ambassador to Spain, the Duke of so-and-so, the Count of so-and-so, Marquis of so-and-so, the Grand Bailiff of the Holy Orders and all that sort of thing, was coming on board to travel with us as far as Naples. I'd read late and slept till noon, when my daughter, Barbara, came knocking at the door. 'Hurry up,' she said, 'there's a duke coming on board.' I said, 'Well, let him.' 'No, no,' she says, 'it's a real duke.' I said, 'Well, what do you want me to do—stop him?' 'Look,' she says, 'I haven't been to Europe before and I'm trying to see it through their eyes, so either you get out of bed, or I'll tell Mom about you going down to second class and sneaking those drinks.' I said, 'I'll be right out.' So we went up on deck, and all the officers were in white uniforms with medals, the band was there, and the velvet ropes, you know, so that he could make his entrance. Pretty soon, a British Admiral's barge sailed up—all polished and everything, flying the British and Italian flags—and out stepped the handsomest man I've ever seen. Boy, he was good looking—jet black hair with these white wings on the sides, and beautifully dressed in a very elegant dark gray suit, with a sort of peculiar looking briefcase attached to his wrist by a silver chain. He came aboard and took the salute—we were in the front row—and as he was walking by, he stopped suddenly, and looked at me. 'Jack!' he yelled. 'How's that sonnafabeech Harry Carey?' And I said, 'Fine, Mario, I guess—but he's dead.' 'What? Harry Carey dead?' 'Yeah.' 'Oh, that's too bad. Nobody told me. And how about that old sonnafabeech Adolphe Menjou?' 'Adolphe's all right.' 'Well, that's good,' he says, 'let's have a drink.' So instead of going through all the protocol, he ducked under the rope, took my arm—my wife couldn't say a word about my taking a drink—and we went down and knocked over three or four whiskies. That was Mario Carillo. He *had* all these titles, you see, but he'd wanted to be

an actor. Barbara was quite put out about the whole damn thing. 'Oh my gosh,' she said, 'a duke—! He's one of Daddy's extra men.' From then on, the nobility ceased to impress her.
How did you move from shorts to features?
Well, we made a five-reel picture [*Straight Shooting*] and they were very upset about it—wanted to cut it down to two—and Mr Laemmle happened to run it. When it was over and they told him it was going to be cut down to two reels, he said, 'Why?' Well, they said, it was only *supposed* to be a two-reeler. And Laemmle said, 'If I order a suit of clothes and the fellow gives me an extra pair of pants free, what am I going to do—throw them back in his face?'

BUCKING BROADWAY (1917)
It was quite novel at the time—instead of riding to the rescue through Western scenery—they rode down Broadway at full tilt, weaving in and out. We went to downtown Los Angeles and rode the cowboys down the streets with a camera car ahead of them. And not a horse slipped.

THE FIGHTING BROTHERS (1919)
Harry went back East on one of those junkets, so I picked up Hoot Gibson and some of the cowboys and we did a two-reeler. We only had two days to do it in, so they never dismounted— the whole thing is on horseback, fast as hell. The head of the studio loved it.

MARKED MEN (1919)
Wasn't it called *Three Godfathers* then?
They changed it to Marked Men *for release.*
They would, the bastards. I remember that picture very well. That's sort of my favourite.
Of the early films?
I think so. I liked the story—that's why I asked to remake it years later [in 1948]. When they originally bought it, the head of the studio hired a guy to write the script—very pompous

fellow, beautifully dressed, white vest, had a lot of ideas—and he started work on a Friday. The man who ran the studio—*not* the executive but the guy who had charge of *making* the pictures—said to us, 'You're going to start shooting Monday.' I said, 'We haven't got the script—the writer just started.' He said, 'The hell with the script—you're all sitting around on your asses drawing a salary—Monday, you start.' So we packed up and went out to the desert. We had one copy of the story—handled it like radium—and made up the picture as we went along. I think we worked three and a half weeks, and *four* weeks after we got *back* this writer they had hired came in with the script. The most beautiful thing you've ever seen—bound in morocco leather and on the top of it in small letters it said *Three Godfathers* and, in big letters, the writer's name. Inside, it was beautifully typed: on the right was the scenario—dialogue, scenes cut up—and on the left were the directions. 'Now, Mr Director, I don't want this, I don't want that.' Beautiful. But it wasn't *Three Godfathers*. Had *nothing* to do with it. The executive producer passed it around the studio, saying, 'This is the way scripts should be,' and meanwhile the damn picture was already shipped. They signed the guy up at $1,000 a week and he never wrote anything again. We found out later he was an insurance agent, had never written a word—just put something over on them.

NORTH OF HUDSON BAY (1924)

We had a sequence of shooting the rapids up in Yosemite. Coming from Maine, I knew a little about canoes, and the only other guy who could use one was Tom Mix, who was brought up near a river in Pennsylvania and could handle a canoe well; but we were the only two. So I had to play the heavy—put on his fur coat and hat—and go down the river with Tom chasing me. There was supposed to be somebody else in-

volved in the chase, so Tom put on *his* clothes. We shot at such a distance, you couldn't tell. It was very funny—I chased Tom, Tom chased me, I chased myself.

THE IRON HORSE (1924)

In general, how closely did you work with writers on the silent films?
We never worked very closely with them. For example, John Russell wrote the original *Iron Horse* and it was really just a simple little story. We went up to Nevada to do it, and when we got up there, it was twenty below zero. All the actors and extras arrived wearing summer clothes; it was great fun—all these boys got up in white knickers—we had a hell of a time. I wish I had time some day to write the story of the making of *The Iron Horse*, because more strange things happened. We put the women in circus cars, and the men had to make their own little homes out of the set. (Later, I remember, we were out in the middle of a desert in Mexico and this little guy named Solly came up to George Schneiderman, the photographer, a wonderful guy to work with, and he says, 'Where's the hotel?' And George says, 'Hotel? You're standing on it.') But the point is we had to spend more and more money and eventually this simple little story came out as a so-called 'epic', the biggest picture Fox had ever made. Of course, if they had known what was going to happen, they never would've let us make it.
Was there quite a lot added to the picture after you finished it?
Not *quite* a lot. But they had this girl whom they were paying a lot of money, and Sol Wurtzel [a Fox executive] said there weren't enough close-ups of her. So they got some other director who put her up against a wall, and she simpered. It had nothing to do with the picture—the lighting didn't match, not even the costume matched.

Still: George O'Brien (left) in The Iron Horse.

They stuck in about twelve of these close-ups, but of course it ruined the picture for me.

Was it the first time that sort of thing happened to you?

Mmhmm. Wasn't the last though.

How did you work with cameramen—Schneiderman, for instance?

Well, I like to have the shadows black and the sunlight white. And I like to put some shadows into the light. We would talk it over, and I'd say 'Right here, George,' and he'd say 'Fine—I'll move a little to the right.' I'd say, 'Go ahead.' We worked together—I never had an argument with a photographer.

Even in the early films, you often liked to shoot from a dark interior to a bright exterior in the same shot.

Yes—it's quite difficult for a cameraman—he has to split his exposure. Usually what you do if a person, for example, walks out of a dark tent into sunlight, you very gently expose for

the exterior as he goes out. You've got to expose just enough so the audience doesn't notice it.

Did you rehearse the actors in the silent days?

You didn't have time for that—all you could tell an actor was where to move, and you could talk to him during the scene—which was a great help. I wish we could now. Sometimes a woman would like a little music—thought it would help her—so I had Danny Borzage play his accordion softly. Everyone did that in those days. It sounds fatuous now, but it really helped.

KENTUCKY PRIDE (1925)

We went to Kentucky to do a little story about horse racing, and we put a lot of comedy into it. There was one little filly—just a beautiful thing —and she had a terrific crush on me. She'd leave the herd and run over and play with me— take my cap, run away with it and look at me— then she'd come back and drop it, and when I'd

Stills: 3 Bad Men. *Above, standing—Frank Campeau, Tom Santschi, O'Brien, McDonald.*

reach down to get the cap, she'd pick it up again and run away. The fellow who owned her said, 'Why don't you name her—she's crazy about you.' So I named her Mary Ford, and she went out and won her first three races easy, then broke down—broke a tendon in her leg or something—and they put her to stud. I'm not a horse racing fan, but I know her get has been famous. I always remember her—she just loved me—very unusual for a horse; I'd be directing the actors or something and she'd come and stand by my chair. Or we'd be leaving—the rest of the herd would be half a mile away—and she'd walk along the fence, following the cars, as far as she could go.

How was Henry B. Walthall to work with?
Oh, great. He was one of the greatest actors of all time—a personality that just leaped out from the screen. He had nothing to do in that picture —but he had such a presence—like Barrymore had, but Walthall was a much better actor.

3 BAD MEN (1926)
That was the first picture I ever made in Jackson Hole. Jack Stone and I wrote the script together, and a lot of it was based on things that had really happened. The villain, played by Lou Tellegen, was taken from an actual character— a man who had been a real dude. There was a land rush in the picture, and several of the people in the company had been in the actual rush—Duke Lee, quite a few of the boys— they'd been kids and rode with their parents—so I talked to them about it. For example, the incident of snatching the baby from under the wheels of a wagon actually happened. And the newspaperman who rode along with his press— printing the news all through the event—that really happened. We did a hell of a land rush;

47

it was on level ground and they whipped the horses up—hundreds of wagons—you could pick them up cheap then—going at full tilt; it was really fast. We did the whole sequence in two days. They cut bits of it into several other pictures—I see it on TV all the time.

MOTHER MACHREE (1927)

I had a lot of fun with that, but you didn't *choose* these things—they were thrown at you and you did the best you could with them. In those days, you'd go to bed at night, and next morning you'd have an early call and you'd find yourself doing another picture. 'What's the name of it?' you'd say. 'We don't know,' they'd say, 'but be down there at seven o'clock.' You didn't know what the hell you were doing, you never got a week's rest to prepare anything, and you never knew who the hell was in it—they had the cast all laid out for you—then occasionally you'd slip your own people in—like J. Farrell McDonald—and they'd steal the picture. One morning, I walked on the set at seven o'clock—

Still: Preparing for the land rush—3 Bad Men.

a lot of actors there I didn't know—and this fellow had a scene in which he was supposed to kiss the girl. So we started to do it and I said to the guy, 'If you're supposed to kiss her, I mean, *kiss* her. Kiss her on the lips. Hold her.' And the actor said, 'But Mr Ford—this is supposed to be my daughter!' 'Oh!' I said. 'Has anybody got the script around here—lemme see the—' After that I usually tried to read the scripts.

FOUR SONS (1928)

Did you choose any of the subjects for the Fox silents?

Still: Earle Foxe plays Hamlet in Upstream.

Well, *Four Sons*. I read the story by Wylie in some magazine, and had them buy it. Strangely enough, it became one of the biggest money makers ever made. It still holds the attendance record at the Roxy, which was one of the biggest theatres in the world. Of course, other pictures have outgrossed it because the admission prices were much lower in those days—a quarter instead of two dollars. I like that picture very much.

John Wayne was the second or third assistant

49

prop man on that film, and I remember we had one very dramatic scene in which the mother had just received notice that one of her sons had died, and she had to break down and cry. It was autumn, the leaves were falling, the woman sitting on a bench in the foreground—a very beautiful scene. We did it two or three times and finally we were getting the perfect take when suddenly in the background comes Wayne, sweeping the leaves up. After a moment, he stopped and looked up with horror. He saw the camera going, dropped the broom and started running for the gate. We were laughing so damn hard—I said, 'Go get him, bring him back.' Fortunately, they finally caught up with him and he came back so sheepfaced. I said, 'All right, it was just an accident.' We were all laughing so much we couldn't work the rest of the day. It was so funny—beautiful scene and this big oaf comes in sweeping the leaves up. He still remembers it.

NAPOLEON'S BARBER (1928)

How did you happen to make your first talkie, Napoleon's Barber?
Because they told me to. It was just a three-reeler—a story about Napoleon stopping on his way to Waterloo to get a shave. Of course, he wouldn't have gone into a barber shop for it—but anyway, he did in this thing. It was the first time anyone ever went outside with a sound system. They said it couldn't be done, and I said, 'Why the hell *can't* it be done?' They said, 'Well, you can't because—' and they gave me a lot of Master's Degree talk, so I said, 'Well, let's try it.' We had Josephine's coach coming across a bridge and the sound men said, 'That'll never do—it's too loud.' But it was perfect—the sound of the horses and the wheels—perfect.
How did you feel about sound at the time?
I didn't feel anything about it—it was just a job of work. Actually, when sound came in we were all fired. They bought up our contracts—sup-

posedly we didn't know anything about sound—and they got a lot of stage directors in from New York. It was a comedy situation: they threw these guys on to the set to make sound pictures—we had schedules of three or four weeks in those days—and after *eight* weeks, these fellows had about a half reel of picture, and the stuff was terrible. They had to hire us all back, only now we wouldn't return unless we got more money. So they increased our salary, and we all came back and said to the actors, 'What are you supposed to say? Well, just *say* it.' And it was perfectly all right, there was nothing to learn—in silent pictures we always had the actors speak the lines they were supposed to say anyway because there were too many lip readers in the audience.

THE BLACK WATCH (1929)

The back-lighting of the battle scenes in The Black Watch *was very effective.*
Well, we never had very many people so I tried that way to make it look as though I had more.
That was another picture they changed after I'd gone. Winfield Sheehan was in charge of production then, and he said there weren't enough love scenes in it. He thought Lumsden Hare was a great British actor—he wasn't, but he impressed Sheehan—so he got Hare to direct some love scenes between McLaglen and Myrna Loy. And they were really horrible—long, talky things, had nothing to do with the story—and completely screwed it up. I wanted to vomit when I saw them.

SALUTE (1929)

The superintendent of Annapolis was from the same island I'm from in Maine—Peak's Island —he and my father were great pals; so we went back there to shoot and they let us do whatever we wanted, turned everything over to us. We put up lights and shot the actual Commencement Ball; after the Ball, we did our close-ups.

Still: The British prisoners in The Black Watch.

The Admirals' daughters were all in the picture—you know, ten bucks a day—and we had a lot of fun.

We brought the entire USC football team back there with us; Ward Bond and Wayne were on it—they were both perfectly natural, so when I needed a couple of fellows to speak some lines, I picked them out and they ended up with parts. Wayne used to work for me during the summertime—labourer, third or fourth prop

man—we all liked him—and then he'd go back to college. Probably that's why I chose him to play this part—I knew him so well. And I was still laughing about him walking into that scene raking up the leaves.

MEN WITHOUT WOMEN (1930)

That was the first submarine picture ever made

Still: Men Without Women *trapped in a submarine.*

actually using a real sub. It was a very effective picture—for those days; these guys are trapped in a submarine and eventually rescued, but one man has to stay behind—one of those things. The submarine leaves from Shanghai, and we had a lot of Chinese atmosphere—the longest bar in the world and so on. I think it was the first picture Dudley Nichols and I did together. From then on, we worked together as much as possible, and I worked very closely with him. He had never written a script before, but he was very good, and he had the same idea I had about paucity of dialogue.

The picture was full of humour despite the tragedy of it. There was one Blue Jacket we had who'd bought a big Chinese vase—and all through the picture he keeps talking about how he's going to bring it back to his Mom. We had a scene in which the rickshaw went over backwards on him—he did a back tumble—and still had a hold of the vase. Even when he goes through the escape hatch, he's still carrying this thing, meaning to bring it back to his mother. It's been copied a lot since.

While we were shooting the rescue scene, a terrific storm came up—the waves were very high—and I said, 'Let's go ahead and do it—what the hell—it's not going to hurt the submarine.' I asked the stuntman to dive overboard and he refused: 'The water's too rough.' So John Wayne, who was playing a bit, says, 'I'll double them all.' And he put on different clothes and dove overboard. J. Farrell McDonald had been on the wagon for years but he'd slipped over to Tijuana and oh, came back drunker than a fiddler's bitch, and nobody would speak to him; so J. Farrell came staggering out on the top deck and looked down. 'What're you doing?' he says. I said, 'I'm supposed to be shooting.' He says, 'The camera going?' I said, 'Yes.' He said, 'I don't want anyone doubling me!' and he did a beautiful dive—forty feet—hit the water, swam out there —he must have been sixty years old at the time. He came back sober . . .

BORN RECKLESS (1930)

It wasn't a good story—something about gangsters—and in the middle of the picture, they go off to war; so we put in a comedy baseball game in France. I was interested in *that*. In those days, when the scripts were dull, the best you could do was to try and get some comedy into it.

UP THE RIVER (1930)

Sheehan wanted to do a great picture about a prison break, so he had some woman write the story and it was just a bunch of junk. Then he went away for a while, and day by day Bill Collier, who was a great character comedian, and I rewrote the script. There was so much opportunity for humour in it that eventually it turned out to be a comedy—all about what went on inside a prison; we had them playing baseball against Sing-Sing, and these two fellows broke back *in* so they'd be in time for the big game. We did it in two weeks; it was Tracy's *and* Bogart's first picture—they were great—just went right in, natural. Sheehan refused to go to the preview, but just at that time all the exhibitors were out here for one of their meetings, and they all went to see it, and they fell out of their chairs. One guy actually *did* fall out of his chair —they had to bring him to. A very funny picture—for those days. I kept ducking the woman who wrote the original script, but she went to another studio on the success of *Up the River* and got three times her salary per script. They tried to remake it some years later—well...

Photograph: Seated on the mast, Joe August (left), Ford, George O'Brien filming Seas Beneath.

SEAS BENEATH (1931)

That was a war story about a Q ship—some good stuff in it—but at the last moment, the head of the studio put a girl who'd never acted before in as the lead because he thought she spoke a few words of German—which she didn't. We had a scene, I remember, in which the German submarine slips up alongside another submarine to refuel, and this girl comes out on to the bridge chewing *gum*! Right in the camera. So we had to go to all the trouble of doing it over again. She just couldn't act. But we did the actual refueling at sea. That stuff

was good and so was the battle stuff, but the story was bad; it was just a lot of hard work, and you couldn't do anything with that girl. Then later they cut the hell out of it.

Seas Beneath marks the first appearance in a talkie of that boastful Irish character of yours who was later personified by McLaglen; is he based on someone you've known?

I suppose the character is a composite of several people. My father, for instance. He would tell

Stills: Above—Ronald Colman, John Qualen, Adele Watson in Arrowsmith *(1931); right— the ' Gold Star Mothers' begin their* Pilgrimage.

about the great things he'd done as a young man, such as the time he lifted a heavy boulder up out of the water, or how he swam Galway Bay. Of course, he was a damn liar, but he would entertain us kids. He was always stopping runaway horses—in fact it was his great

yen; it was all horses and buggies in those days and, like a bullfighter, he stopped a horse and grabbed it—he was a big, powerful man—and yanked this horse to its knees.

THE BRAT (1931)
That was just one of those damn things they handed you, but we had a fight between these two women—and it turned into a real one— they hated each other's guts and really went at

it. I was going to stop it, and then I said, 'The hell with it, let 'em go, nobody's gonna get hurt.' Pulling hair and slugging one another— there was no faking about it. Very funny.

DR BULL (1933)
Did you improvise a lot with Will Rogers on Dr Bull?
Well, no writer could write for Will Rogers, so I'd say to him, 'This is the script but this is not

you—the words will be false coming from you. Just learn the sense of it, and say it in your own words.' Some of the lines he'd speak from the script, but most of the time he'd make up his own; he'd stop and let people pick up their cues and then go on; he wouldn't write the lines down, but he'd work it out beforehand and then just get in front of the camera and get the sense of the scene in his own inimitable way. *Dr Bull* was a downbeat story, but Bill managed to get a lot of humour into it—and it became a hell of a good picture. It was one of Bill's favourites. We did three pictures together and it was always a

Photograph: Ford, Will Rogers on Dr Bull. *Still: Karloff, McLaglen, W. Ford in* The Lost Patrol.

lot of fun working for Bill. *Judge Priest* turned out very well too, it was very funny; *Steamboat Round the Bend* should have been a great picture but at that time they had a change of studio and a new manager came in who wanted to show off, so he recut the picture, and took all the comedy out.

THE LOST PATROL (1934)
It was a character study—you got to know the

57

life story of each of the men. We shot it at Yuma in two weeks. When you're shooting in the desert, if you track up the sand, you can't retake—you've got to move to another location. I had a shot of the British cavalry coming in to rescue the lone survivor—we had a lovely location, it was about 5:30 in the afternoon and there were these long shadows of the horses lined up—it was very beautiful. Suddenly a plane swooped down over them and the horses scattered, made a mess of the sand. I was furious. There was no point in trying to get another location and get the men back in their places, because the light would be gone—it was too late. When we got to the airfield, which was close by, it turned out to have been the producer's plane. This was his first picture; he'd been an exhibitor, and the head of the studio was a friend of his so he asked me, 'Do you mind taking him as a producer?' and I said, 'No, he's all right, I like him, he's kind of a nice guy.' Now he steps out of the

plane with a big cigar in his mouth and he says, 'Did you see us come in?' I said, 'You son-of-a-bitch, you've cost us half a day's work.' He says, 'Why? I thought I'd give you a kick.' I said, 'You sure as hell did!'

When you're shooting on the desert, you start work at 6:30, work until 11:00 and then go to the camp, which is nearby, and have lunch—if anybody wants lunch; then you'd get in the shade and start work again at 2:30, because until then it would be so hot—110, sometimes 120 degrees—a man couldn't stand it. Well, the producer got me aside and he said, 'Look, I've been figuring it out. I know you stop work from 11:00 to 2:30. Eleven, twelve, one, two,' he says, 'multiply that by seven—how many hours have you got?' I said, 'I'm no good at arithmetic.' He says, 'Seven times three and one-half—well, around 21 hours. That's three or four days work.' I said, 'But you can't work in the heat.' 'Jack,' he said, 'it's great. I've never felt so good in my life.' He just dropped out of the sky, you know, and he's still smoking a cigar. 'For once,' he says, 'work till twelve and take half an hour for lunch. Look at all the time you'll save—you'll be out of here quicker.' I said, 'We're doing all right the way we are. I'm not going to have a lot of sick people on my hands—sunstroke and everything else.' 'But this air is great,' he says, and he goes out there bare-headed—walking around and shaking hands—really the big shot. 'I feel great,' he says, 'getting away, you know.' About an hour later, I wanted to talk to him: 'Where's Mr. So-and-so?' They looked at me. I said, 'Yes, where is he?' They said, 'Sorry, but they just took him to the hospital with sunstroke.' I went down to the hospital in Yuma to see him; God, he was the sickest man I've ever

Stills: The Whole Town's Talking (*1935*): *Edward G. Robinson as killer* (left, with Jean Arthur) *and as clerk* (right, with the press).

58

He won't do a Western—' And Joe says, 'An Irish story? That ought to be good, why don't you let him do it? Will it cost much?' I said, 'No, it's a cheap little story.' So he said to the other fellows, 'Well, let him do that and in the meantime you can find a Western for him.'

Just around that time, producers were coming in, and they handed the story to another famous name, who didn't want to have anything to do with it; they went through four producers, and finally we picked the same guy we had on *The Lost Patrol*. I said, 'You're the producer of this thing.' He said, 'Gee, what is it about?' I said,

'Well, read it.' He says, 'Oh, I never read books —I just don't have time to.' I said, 'What do you mean "don't have time to?" What do you do in the afternoon? Now you just go to a bar, sit in the corner, open the book and read it.' But he never did.

Now the studio was pretty sore about the whole thing and after we'd been working a week

Stills: The Informer (*1935*)—*Victor McLaglen (below) with prostitutes in a deleted sequence and (right) with Wallace Ford.*

Joe Kennedy sold the company and they stopped the picture. Then they considered: 'Well, we've got so-and-so much money in it and it's not costing much' (it cost a little over $200,000 —we made it in under three weeks) 'we've got these people under contract'; so finally they decided, 'Oh, go ahead.' But they wouldn't let me work on the lot—they sent me across the street to a dusty old stage, which was great because I was alone and they didn't bother me. They wouldn't build us any real sets though— the city of Dublin was just painted canvas.

We went ahead and did the picture, and when they showed it in New York, it got rave reviews. Now suddenly all these producers came back and tried to get their names put on it: 'Produced by—' But by then the prints had been made, and so it went out without their names on it and they were furious. I was pretty sore about the whole thing myself.

But I enjoyed making it. We were looking at the rushes and I asked the producer, 'Did you see when Wally Ford was shot and went out the window?' He said, 'Oh, yes.' I said, 'Could you hear the scratching of his nails on the window-sill as he went down?' He says, 'Oh, yes—but

made right on the set. I said. 'Victor, interrupt —say, "You're a liar, you're a liar"—you know, interrupt whenever you want to. There are no lines in the script I can give you, but just realize they've got you, and try to lie your way out of it.' Preston Foster's a pretty good actor and I told him, 'Help Victor all you can, ad lib a little bit, throw him a few lines, interrupt *him*.' It went pretty well.

THE PLOUGH AND THE STARS (1937)
After I'd finished the picture, another studio head said, 'Why make a picture where a man and woman are married? The main thing about pictures is love or sex. Here you've got a man and woman married at the start—who's interested in that?' So after I left, he sent an assistant

Stills: Mary of Scotland. Left—Mary Stuart goes to her martyrdom.

was pretty cloudy—it had been raining—but the clouds were so nice, and they had that occasional streak of light. Ordinarily, we would have knocked off for the day, but I had a great cameraman, Artie Miller, and I said, 'We've got to do something with the weather, with these clouds.' I said, 'We've got everybody here—let's bury Victor!' And Artie said, 'That's a swell idea. I'll open up the exposure a bit—we'll get a good effect.' So we put in the funeral.

Stills: The Hurricane *with C. Aubrey Smith, Mary Astor, Raymond Massey and (right) Dorothy Lamour.*

THE HURRICANE (1937)

Did Goldwyn interfere with you on The Hurricane?

It's a funny thing, Sam Goldwyn never interfered with anybody. As a matter of fact, he very seldom visited the set. But when they ran *The Hurricane* for him, he said, 'It isn't personalized enough'—an expression I didn't quite understand but when I figured it out, I agreed with him. Our time and budget had run out, you see, and I had just done what was in the script. So after he said that, I went back and worked five or six days and put in some closer shots.

FOUR MEN AND A PRAYER (1938)

You seemed to have a tongue-in-the-cheek attitude about all that British stiff-upper-lip business in Four Men and a Prayer.

Oh, I don't know—I just didn't like the story, or anything else about it, so it was a job of work. I kidded them slightly.

SUBMARINE PATROL (1938)

Having been a Blue Jacket—though I wasn't in the submarine fleet—I had a lot of sympathy for them, I knew what they went through. The head of the fleet was an old pal of mine and he helped me on it. I had a lot of fun with that picture and, of course, all the comedy in it wasn't in the script; we put it in as we went along.

STAGECOACH (1939)

I still like that picture. It was really *Boule-de-suif*, and I imagine the writer, Ernie Haycox, got his idea from there and turned it into a Western story which he called 'Stage to Lordsburg.'

How did you find Monument Valley?

I knew about it. I had travelled up there once, driving through Arizona on my way to Santa

I usually break the conventional rules—sometimes deliberately.

Frank Nugent was once talking to me about that film and he said, 'Only one thing I can't understand about it, Jack—in the chase, why didn't the Indians just shoot the horses pulling the stagecoach?' And I said, 'In actual fact that's probably what *did* happen, Frank, but if they had, it would have been the end of the picture, wouldn't it?'

YOUNG MR LINCOLN (1939)

Everybody knows Lincoln was a great man, but the idea of the picture was to give the feeling that even as a young man you could sense there was going to be something great about this man. I had read a good deal about Lincoln, and we tried to get some comedy into it too, but everything in the picture was true. Lamar Trotti was a good writer and we wrote it together.

They cut some nice things out of it. For example, I had a lovely scene in which Lincoln rode into town on a mule, passed by a theatre and stopped to see what was playing, and it was the Booth Family doing *Hamlet*; we had a typical old-fashioned poster up. Here was this

poor shabby country lawyer wishing he had enough money to go see *Hamlet* when a very handsome young boy with dark hair—you knew he was a member of the Booth Family—fresh, snobbish kid, all beautifully dressed—just walked out to the edge of the plank walk and looked at Lincoln. He looked at this funny, incongruous man in a tall hat riding a mule, and you knew there was some connection there. They cut it out—too bad.

Stills: 'Everything in the picture was true'—Henry Fonda in Young Mr Lincoln.

I just liked it, that's all. I'd read the book—it was a good story—and Darryl Zanuck had a good script on it. The whole thing appealed to me—being about simple people—and the story was similar to the famine in Ireland, when they threw the people off the land and left them wandering on the roads to starve. That may have had something to do with it—part of my Irish tradition—but I liked the idea of this family going out and trying to find their way in

Stills: The Joads—Pa (Russell Simpson), Uncle John (Frank Darien), Ma (Jane Darwell), Rosasharn (Dorris Bowdon) and, above, with Tom (Fonda).

the world. It was a timely story. It's still a good picture—I saw part of it on TV recently.

Gregg Toland did a great job of photography there—absolutely nothing but nothing to photograph, not *one* beautiful thing in there— just sheer good photography. I said to him,

TOBACCO ROAD (1941)

Would you have changed Tobacco Road *even if the play hadn't had censorship problems?*

Did the play have censorship problems? Oh, the girl. Well, we suggested that, but I think we did it nicely. I don't think it offended anybody. I enjoyed making the picture. I saw it on television recently and enjoyed it again. Poor Charlie Grapewin was a fine actor, and a wonderful guy to work with, always cracking

jokes and playing practical jokes, and then he'd go and get right into his part again.

SEX HYGIENE (1941)

Darryl Zanuck was a reserve officer and he said to me, 'This would just be for the Army—but these kids have got to be taught about these things. It's horrible—do you mind doing it?' So I said, 'Sure, what the hell, I'll do it.' And it was easy to make—we did it in two or three days. It really *was* horrible; not being for general release, we could do anything—we had guys out there with VD and everything else. I think it made its point and helped a lot of young kids. I looked at it and threw up.

HOW GREEN WAS MY VALLEY (1941)

Was How Green Was My Valley *the first time you brought the characters back at the end—the way you did later in* The Long Gray Line *and* The Quiet Man?

I believe so. I wanted to reprise the mother's song so I got the idea of bringing the cast back. In the theatre I always like to see the cast come out—regardless of whether the guy's playing the messenger boy or the butler—I like to see him come out and take his bow. That's probably where I got the idea.

Was the family life personal to you?

Well, I'm the youngest of thirteen, so I suppose the same things happened to me—I was a fresh young kid at the table.

Was much of that film made up on the set?

Phil Dunne wrote the script and we stuck pretty close to it. There may have been a few things added, but that's what a director is for. You can't just have people stand up and say their lines—there has to be a little movement, a little action, little bits of business and things.

Publicity photographs: Gene Tierney, with Ward Bond, in Tobacco Road.

a kiss at the finish—I've never done that. Of course, they *were* glorious in defeat in the Philippines—they kept on fighting.

MY DARLING CLEMENTINE (1946)

I knew Wyatt Earp. In the very early silent days, a couple of times a year, he would come up to visit pals, cowboys he knew in Tombstone; a lot of them were in my company. I

Photograph (left): Ford, with Hedda Hopper, shooting They Were Expendable. *Still: Wyatt Earp and the Clantons in* My Darling Clementine.

think I was an assistant prop boy then and I used to give him a chair and a cup of coffee, and he told me about the fight at the O. K. Corral. So in *My Darling Clementine*, we did it exactly the way it had been. They didn't just walk up the street and start banging away at each other; it was a clever military manoeuvre.

THE FUGITIVE (1947)

It came out the way I wanted it to—that's why it's one of my favourite pictures—to me, it was perfect. It wasn't popular. The critics got at it, and evidently it had no appeal to the public, but I was very proud of my work. There are some things in it that I've seen repeated a million times in other pictures and on television—so at least it had that effect. It had a lot of damn good photography—with those black and white shadows. We had a good cameraman, Gabriel Figueroa, and we'd *wait* for the light—instead of the way it is nowadays where regardless of the light, you shoot.
Did you alter the Graham Greene novel quite a bit?
Not quite a bit, but you couldn't do the original

Stills: below, Tombstone in My Darling Clementine; *right ,* The Fugitive, *Dolores Del Rio.*

funny.

Well, that was my racket for a while, and there wasn't anything funny about it. I wonder what s.o.b. will be the first to make a comedy about Vietnam?

WAGON MASTER (1950)

I wrote the original story. Along with *The Fugitive* and *The Sun Shines Bright*, I think *Wagon Master* came closest to being what I had wanted to achieve.

THIS IS KOREA (1951)

Your documentary of the Korean War was very grim, especially compared to Midway *or* They Were Expendable.

Stills: Three Godfathers *with (top left)* Ward Bond, Jane Darwell; *(top centre)* Mildred Natwick, Wayne, Harry Carey, Jr., Pedro Armendariz. *Bottom left—*She Wore A Yellow Ribbon *Right, top and bottom—*Wagon Master.

could put it in—like Barry Fitzgerald bringing the crib into their bedroom on the morning after the wedding night, and seeing the broken bed. That was just taking advantage of the situation. Nobody has ever heard what he says when he comes in there, you know—because the laugh is too loud. Hundreds of people have asked me—'what did he say?' I never can figure it out. ['Impetuous—Homeric . . .'] But that condition still exists in Connemara—where my people came from—the wife is supposed to come to her husband with a 'dot' or dowry—a few pounds or something—it's a good thing.

Then you agree with her feelings in the film?
I just thought it was good drama. The only mistake we made was having him throw the money on the fire—he should have tossed it to one of the fellows and said, 'Give it to charity' or something—

I thought it was a great gesture.
Yes, well, who would he give it to anyway? Not the parish priest—he has more money than the Lord Mayor of Dublin.

THE SUN SHINES BRIGHT (1953)

The Sun Shines Bright, like Wagon Master, *seems to be a film you did for yourself.*
That's true. I knew they weren't going to be smash hits—I did them for my own amusement. And it didn't hurt anybody—they didn't *make* any money, but they always got their initial cost back. *The Sun Shines Bright* is my favourite picture—I love it. And it's true to life, it happened. Irvin Cobb got everything he wrote from real life, and that's the best of his Judge Priest stories.

Has it become increasingly difficult to do a picture for yourself like that?
Oh, you can't anymore—it's impossible. You've got to go through a series of commands now and you never know who the hell reads the scripts any more. You can't get an O.K. here in Hollywood for a script—it's got to go back to New

Photograph: directing The Sun Shines Bright.

York, and through a president and a board of directors and bankers and everybody else. What I used to do was try and make a big picture, a smash, and then I could palm off a little one on them. You can't do it any more.

THE LONG GRAY LINE (1955)

Would you agree that The Long Gray Line *is the story of a failure who succeeded in ways he couldn't see?*
That's true, yes. He was a real character—grew up at West Point and knew Eisenhower and Wiedemeier, and all those people—wonderful old guy.

Again it's your theme of 'the glory in defeat.'
Well, I'd hardly use such an academic or poetic title—although it is a good expression. As a matter of fact, you may attribute it to me if you wish—because I may use it anyway.

How did you like CinemaScope?

91

Stills: Peter Graves, Tyrone Power (above) in The Long Grey Line; Ava Gardner (left) in Mogambo.

I hated it. You've never seen a painter use that kind of composition—even in the great murals, it still wasn't this huge tennis court. Your eyes pop back and forth, and it's very difficult to get a close-up.

MISTER ROBERTS (1955)
A lot of my stuff was cut out by the producer, Leland Hayward, because it wasn't in the original play. Then Josh Logan, who wrote the play, looked at the stuff that had been cut and he said, 'This is funny stuff, for Pete's sake,' and insisted on putting a lot of it back in.

THE SEARCHERS (1956)
It's the tragedy of a loner. He's the man who came back from the Civil War, probably went

Still: ' He could never really be part of the family '— Wayne as Ethan in The Searchers.

over into Mexico, became a bandit, probably fought for Juarez or Maximilian—probably Maximilian, because of the medal. He was just a plain loner—could never really be a part of the family.

Was that the meaning of the door opening on him at the start and closing at the end?

Mmhmm.

Was the scene, toward the beginning, during which Wayne's sister-in-law gets his coat for him, meant to convey silently a past love between them?

Well, I thought it was pretty obvious—that his brother's wife was in love with Wayne; you couldn't hit it on the nose, but I think it's very plain to anyone with any intelligence. You could tell from the way she picked up his cape and I think you could tell from Ward Bond's

expression and from his exit—as though he
hadn't noticed anything.

*The Indians are always given great dignity in
your films.*

It's probably an unconscious impulse—but they
are a very dignified people—even when they
were being defeated. Of course, it's not very
popular in the United States. The audience
likes to see Indians get killed. They don't consider them as human beings—with a great

Stills: Jeffrey Hunter, Vera Miles (left) in The
Searchers; *Wayne (right and below) in* The
Wings of Eagles.

culture of their own—quite different from ours. If you analyzed the thing carefully, however, you'd find that their religion is very *similar* to ours.

THE WINGS OF EAGLES (1957)

The Wings of Eagles is once again the tragedy of a man who never really got what he wanted. Life disappointed him. But he *did* devise the baby carrier: they were not fighting ships, but

Stills: 'Spig' Wead and a film he wrote—Ford's Air Mail (*1932*) *with Ralph Bellamy, Slim Summerville.*

95

supply ships that carried planes to replace the ones lost in battle on the big carriers. Spig Wead put that programme over.

I didn't want to do the picture because Spig was a great pal of mine. But I didn't want any-one *else* to make it. I knew him first when he was deck officer, black shoe, with the old Mississippi—before he went in for flying. I was out of the Navy then and I used to go out and see him and some of the other officers. Spig was always interested in writing and I helped him a bit, encouraged him. We did a couple of pic-tures together. He died in my arms.

I tried to tell the story as truthfully as possi-ble, and everything in the picture was true. The fight in the club—throwing the cake—actually happened; I can verify that as an eye witness— I ducked it. I thought it was very funny when they all fell into the pool; that actually happened —they ran like hell through the kitchen and all landed in the pool. And the plane landing in the

96

Stills: Rising of the Moon (*left*); Last Hurrah (*above*); Horse Soldiers (*right*); Sgt. Rutledge (*bottom right*).

swimming pool—right in the middle of the Admiral's tea—that really happened.

The title was lousy—I screamed at that. I just wanted to call it *The Spig Wead Story*, but they said 'Spig' is a funny name, and people are going to wonder who's Spig Wead.
Wasn't Ward Bond playing you in the picture?
I didn't intend it that way, but *he* did. I woke up one morning and my good hat was gone, my pipe and everything else; they'd taken all the Academy Awards and put them in the office set.

THE LAST HURRAH (1958)

The Last Hurrah again deals with a defeat.
What do you call it—'the glory in defeat'? Right. O.K. I liked that picture very much. It was a good character study. And Tracy was a wonderful guy to work with.

THE HORSE SOLDIERS (1959)

I don't think I ever saw it. But a lot of the things in it actually happened—such as the children from the Military Academy marching out against the Union soldiers—that happened several times.

SERGEANT RUTLEDGE (1960)

Was the point of Sergeant Rutledge *that the Negro's home was the Army?*

Yes, that's the point. The Negro soldier, the regular, is very proud. They had always been a cavalry outfit, but in this last war, they were mechanized—they took their horses away, and they were broken-hearted. They were very proud of their outfit; they had great esprit de corps. I liked that picture. It was the first time we had ever shown the Negro as a hero.

TWO RODE TOGETHER (1961)

I didn't like the story, but I did it as a favour to

Harry Cohn, who was stuck with the project and said, 'Will you do this for me?' I said, 'Good God, this is a lousy script.' He said, 'I know it, but we're pledged for it—we're all set—we've got Widmark and Stewart signed up.' I said, 'O.K., I'll do the damn thing.' And I didn't enjoy it. I just tried to make Stewart's character as humorous as possible.

His morality was a little ambiguous.
Isn't all our morality a little ambiguous?

When possible do you like to play a scene through in one angle, without cutting it up, as you did in the scene by the river between Stewart and Widmark?
Well, it's better if you can do that, if you get close enough so the audience can see the faces clearly. Certain directors go by fixed rules—they

Still: Richard Widmark and James Stewart in the scene by the river from Two Rode Together.

say you must have a close-up of everything. But we've got this big screen: instead of putting a lot of pock-marked faces on it—big horrible head, eye—I just don't like it—if I can play a scene in a two-shot, where you can see both faces very well, I prefer it that way. You see people instead of just faces. Of course, nowadays in pictures, you never even get a chance to look at anyone's face. I watched something the other night with Sophia Loren in it; well, she's a nice woman to look at—but she was always hidden by somebody or her face would just peek out. Here she was playing the lead, and the camera panned away from her all the time and you never did get a good look at Sophia. That's new direction. It's a funny thing, these kids get out here from New York, stage directors, and the first thing they do when they get here, they forget the story, forget the people, forget the characters, forget the dialogue and they concentrate on this new, wonderful toy, the camera.

You never cover a scene from many angles.
No—because the actors get tired, they get jaded and lose the spontaneity—so that they're just mouthing words. But if you get the first or second take, there's a sparkle, an uncertainty about it; they're not sure of their lines, and it gives you a sense of nervousness and suspense.
Do you also avoid shooting a lot of coverage so that producers won't have the material to re-edit?
No, I've always done that—because film is very expensive and I hate to waste it—I was brought up that way. It's not so they can't change it, because they *can*—and *do*—take it back to New York and cut up the most dramatic scenes.

THE MAN WHO SHOT LIBERTY VALANCE (1962)

Toward the start of Liberty Valance, *when Vera Miles comes to Wayne's burned-out house, isn't the music the Ann Rutledge theme from* Young Mr Lincoln?

Yes, it was the same; we bought it from Al Newman. I love it—one of my favourite tunes —one I can hum. Generally, I hate music in pictures—a little bit now and then, at the end or the start—but something like the Ann Rutledge theme *belongs*. I don't like to see a man alone in the desert, dying of thirst, with the Philadelphia Orchestra behind him.

Still: ' Maybe I'm getting older '—*Stewart, Vera Miles in* The Man Who Shot Liberty Valance.

One feels that your sympathy in Liberty Valance *is with John Wayne and the Old West.*
Well, Wayne actually played the lead; Jimmy Stewart had most of the scenes, but Wayne was the central character, the motivation for the whole thing. I don't know—I liked them both— I think they were both good characters and I rather liked the story, that's all. I'm a hardnosed director; I get a script—if I like it, I'll do

Stills: 'Print the Legend'—The Man Who Shot Liberty Valance—*Wayne and Stewart with (above) Woody Strode, Vera Miles and (right) with Edmond O'Brien.*

it. Or if I say, 'Oh, this is all right'—I'll do it. If I don't like it, I'll turn it down.

By the end of the picture, though, it seemed very clear that Vera Miles was still in love with Wayne.

Well, we meant it that way.

Your picture of the West has become increasingly sad over the years—like the difference in mood, for example, between Wagon Master *and* Liberty Valance.

Possibly—I don't know—I'm not a psychologist. Maybe I'm getting older.

DONOVAN'S REEF (1963)

Is the life pictured in Donovan's Reef *a kind you might have liked for yourself?*

No, not at all, I wouldn't like to live on an island. I like to go to Honolulu for a couple of weeks on leave, but after that, the island closes in on me. Of course, I know guys who've done exactly that, and are still in the South Seas— own old sea saloons, and doing very well— thirty or forty Navy children, five or six Navy

wives. But it's not the life for me.

Was that moment when Mae Marsh blows the man's cigar ash off the table something you added on the set?

Yes, well, the writer knew nothing about Boston, and I certainly do know Boston and those people. Half of them are half-witted and half of them are bright, but there's always a couple of kooks among them.

HOW THE WEST WAS WON (1962)

How did you like Cinerama on How the West Was Won?

It's worse than CinemaScope, because the ends curl on moving shots and the audience moves

Stills (left): relationships in Donovan's Reef— *between Michael Patrick 'Guns' Donovan (Wayne), Thomas Aloysius 'Boats' Gilhooley (Lee Marvin), and their ladies (Elizabeth Allen and Dorothy Lamour).*

instead of the picture. You have to hold onto your chair. I didn't care for it.

CHEYENNE AUTUMN (1964)
I had wanted to make it for a long time. I've killed more Indians than Custer, Beecher and Chivington put together, and people in Europe always want to know about the Indians. There are two sides to every story, but I wanted to show their point of view for a change. Let's face it, we've treated them very badly—it's a blot on our shield; we've cheated and robbed, killed, murdered and massacred and everything else, but they kill one white man and, God, out come the troops.
Do you make it a practice never to rehearse an action sequence?
You can't—it looks phoney. You can never tell what will happen—one man's liable to fall, the horse is liable to fall. No, I'm an old hard-nosed director who never rehearsed action.

Stills: above: filling a mass grave after the Battle of Shiloh in How the West Was Won; *right—Dodge City interlude in* Cheyenne Autumn.

Was Cheyenne Autumn *changed considerably from the way you had planned it?*
Yes.
Could you say some of the things that were changed?
No, I don't remember. But there were things even before we started shooting. Carroll Baker is a wonderful girl and a wonderful actress— I'm very fond of her—but I wanted to do it right: the woman who did go with the Indians was a middle-aged spinster who finally dropped out because she couldn't take it any more. But you couldn't do that—you had to have a young, beautiful girl.
Was the score the one you wanted?
No, I thought it was a bad score and there was too much of it—didn't need it. Just like in *The*

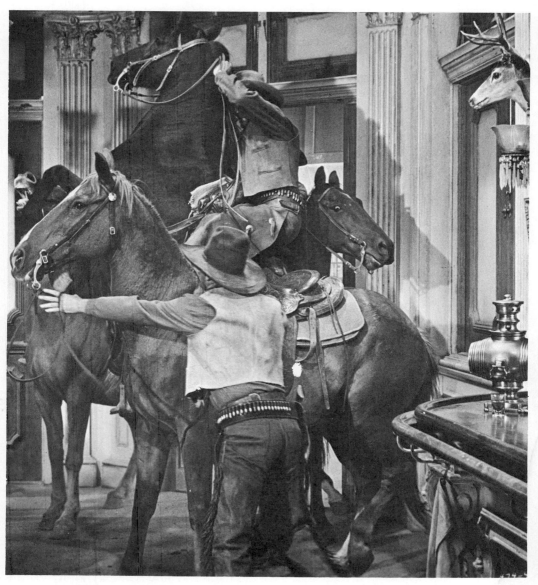

Searchers: with that music they should have been Cossacks instead of Indians.

Did you intend the Dodge City sequence as a kind of intermission, as well as a satiric comment on 'the Battle of Dodge City'?

Yes. It actually happened that way. They were a load of easterners—not many cowboys there—and they went out thinking they were going to pick up a scalp or something. Someone fired a shot, and they all ran like hell. [In initial engagements, the studio ruined the effect of this 'intermission'—a comedy sequence in the midst of an otherwise tragic story—by arbitrarily

placing an actual intermission in the middle of it. In subsequent engagements of the film, the point of the sequence was obliterated when the entire second half showing 'the Battle of Dodge City' (which had followed the studio's intermission) was deleted.—P.B.]

YOUNG CASSIDY (1965)

How had you planned to end Young Cassidy?

Well, after the play was over, and after Maggie Smith had left—while he was standing there in the rain outside the theatre—I wanted Julie Christie, by now a streetwalker, to come over to

106

Stills: Young Cassidy—' *I only did . . . some scenes between Julie and Rod Taylor.'*

him and say, 'Oh, Sean, I loved it—it was wonderful—you ought to be proud of yourself. God bless you.' It took this poor little tart to appreciate what he'd done. And she walks away, disappears in the rain, leaving him there. The producers told me why it shouldn't be done that way, but I argued with them, and they promised to do it after I got sick and left. But they didn't. It would have kicked the damn story up.

7 WOMEN (1966)

Did you have a lot of interference on 7 Women?
Yes.

Was it re-cut after you finished with it?
I presume so, I don't know—I never saw it. When I left, it was cut beautifully. I think it was a good story. And it was a good switch for me, to turn around and make a picture all about women. It didn't do well here, but it was a sensation in Europe. I thought it was a hell of a good picture.

Why does Bancroft sacrifice herself for the others?
I think that's a rather naive question, Peter. She was a doctor—her object in life was to save people. She was a woman who had no religion, but she got in with this bunch of kooks and started acting like a human being.

Has it been more difficult recently to get a good script?
Well, there's no such thing as a good script really. Scripts are dialogue, and I don't like all that *talk*. I've always tried to get things across visually. I don't like to do books or plays. I prefer to take a short story and expand it, rather than take a novel and try to condense. But it *has* become more difficult to get a good *story*.

How have you usually worked a writer?
I spend the afternoon with him and work out a sequence; we talk and argue back and forth—he suggests something, I suggest something. That night or the next morning, he knocks it out on his typewriter, blocks it out, and we see whether we were right or wrong. I usually like to have a writer on the set—I always did with Nichols—but you can't any more—the companies won't pay the expense.

Do you have them put in the shots, or just the basic sequence?
Oh, just the sequence—I ask them to dump the cutting up—and just put down what happens and dialogue. They don't say, 'scene so-and-so, camera moves in, zooms in, pans—' None of that stuff, because it's none of their business.

How long after you started making pictures did you come to feel that what you were doing was something important?

Well, that's a presumption I can't accept. I never felt that way about it. I've always enjoyed making pictures—it's been my whole life. I like the people I'm around—I don't mean the higher echelons—I mean the actors, the actresses, the grips, the electricians. I like those people. I like to be on the set and, regardless of what the story is, I like to work in pictures—it's fun.

Harry Carey tutored me in the early years, sort of brought me along, and the only thing I always had was an eye for composition—I don't know where I got it—and that's all I *did* have. As a kid, I thought I was going to be an artist; I used to sketch and paint a great deal and I think, for a kid, I did pretty good work—at least I received a lot of compliments about it. But I have never thought about what I was doing in terms of art, or 'this is great', or 'world-shaking', or anything like that. To me, it was always a job of work—which I enjoyed immensely—and that's it.

Still: 7 Women—'*A hell of a good picture.*'

4 TAPS

I knew he was dying and that if I didn't drive down to see him before leaving for Rome to make the new picture there was a good chance he would be gone before we returned. It was the middle of June, 1973. About six months earlier the Fords had sold their house in Bel Air and moved to one in Palm Desert. I don't believe it was really something they were anxious to do, but economic considerations prevailed. After all, Jack hadn't made a picture since 1965— though for at least six of those years he had been most capable of one—and conditions weren't getting any better. I had phoned him a few times since the move and spoke with him briefly the night the American Film Institute gave the director their first Life Achievement Award and President Nixon presented him with the Medal of Freedom, which is the highest civilian honor our country can bestow.

Highlights of that evening were subsequently seen on a television special which managed only to emphasize the least attractive and most commercial aspects of the affair. But that's another story—the vulgarity of the actual evening itself was far outweighed, if you were there, by the sheer fascination of it. There was hardly a face in the crowd you couldn't recognize—more stars and directors and producers came out than I have ever seen at the Oscars—though a few of the more politically minded protested the Nixon presence by *not* coming. Jane Fonda, I believe, even picketed. But then, that was her main occupation those days, as well as her privilege, though one might wish she would stop mixing politics with art quite so ferociously. Nixon was honoring a great artist that night—the first time a film personality had been so recognized —and he was present not as one particular president one did not admire or respect, but rather as the highest elected representative of the nation acknowledging the achievement of a lifetime—an opus that includes not only Miss Fonda's father's best films, but some of the finest pictures anyone's ever been in. So she shouldn't have picketed. In fact, it would have been elegant to come—a significant sign, indeed, that despite the presence of a politician she detested, the attention being paid to a major artist in her own chosen field was more important. But no doubt there were reservations too about John Ford's own politics. As if it mattered really what a humanist poet of Ford's dimension and depth thought about the issues of our day. His best movies—and there are many of them— are for *all* our days. They are the size of legends and possess the soul of myth. Orson Welles said it once: "John Ford knows what the earth is made of."

I wanted the whole town there that night because I knew it would be the last time they could see him and the last time he could see them. So, what the hell, pull out all the stops! The Marine Band and the television schmaltz and all the junk. It was Jack Ford's last hurrah. The funny thing is—and this is only a feeling of mine—I do not believe finally that *he* cared very much. Certainly he made damn sure to get through the evening all right—a great effort, for he was already very ill by then; he made the appropriate speech and the proper signs of emotion. He shook his head in disbelief at the honors being paid to him and even brushed away a tear. But I could swear the tear was not there and the rest of it just a gallant performance. He was too much of a showman to let his audience down—and he had staged scenes of this nature enough times in his films to know how the lead should perform. One could always imagine Ford showing Tyrone Power how to play the last sequence of *The Long Gray Line* as well as giving John Wayne some ideas for the end of *She Wore a Yellow Ribbon*—but never more sharply than in the way Jack behaved that night under the lights. Still, he had staged these things so much better himself—made them so moving on the screen—how could anyone compete with the master's own evocation of the glory in defeat, the pathos of the last stand? He knew he was dying and that none of this really mattered; he had created what he could, and all the rest was show. If he can hear me now, perhaps he is cursing my words, but there must be a private laugh behind the profanity, because Mr Ford had the devil in him, thank God for that.

On the way to the new Ford home in Palm Desert, I picked up Howard Hawks in Palm Springs; he wanted to come along, though he had already been several times. Jack was in bed —most of the times I had seen him during the ten years I knew him, he had been in bed—it was his own particular office—but it was a shock to see him this time. There was physically so little of him left. Like some horrible parasite, the cancer seemed to have shrunk him by half. He looked not 78 but 110. Hawks, by comparison—and he is only a year younger—looked a youthful 50.

All great directors are great actors first. And no one more than Ford. I came into the room a flash too early and caught him hurriedly getting his cigar lighted so as to strike a pose of casual ease—as though nothing in the world was wrong, just an afternoon visit with a couple of friends. And that's how he behaved; whenever you asked how he felt, the answer was always, "Pretty well," with no melodrama, no false bravery. There was never any talk of fatal illness or pain —and his daughter Barbara told me he did not even ask for the pain-killing pills until less than two weeks before he succumbed. The chat was short and typical of many others we had had— except that it was so awful to see him as he looked then, trying so valiantly not to let us notice. He kidded me, as he always did, for making every sentence of mine a question. Hawks, who is usually most reserved and restrained, came on like a college boy before his favorite professor —it was touching, his grace and charm. (I remember I asked him once if he'd been influenced by Ford in making his first Western, *Red River,* and he said he didn't know how anyone could make a Western without being influenced by John Ford. The funny thing is that many people to this day think that Ford directed *Red River,* since it *is* a famous Western and John Wayne is in it. And whenever someone mistakenly complimented Ford on *Red River,* he would say, quite casually, "Thank you very much." Hawks himself delighted in telling that story.

"Your five minutes are up," Ford said, and that meant it was time to go. We left. From

Still: John Ford in Monument Valley for the last time, during production of Directed by John Ford.

Rome, I called him several times. The conversations were short and friendly, but he sounded weaker each time. He died on a Friday. The Monday of that week was the last time I spoke with him, and when I heard his voice I knew he didn't have long—he sounded so frail. If you had seen or heard him on the set, in control of 600 actors and technicians, it would have broken your heart. "Pretty well," he said again, but with considerable effort. Hawks saw him on Tuesday. On Wednesday Ford said he wanted to see "Duke," and Thursday Wayne flew down and spent a while with him.

"Come for the deathwatch, Duke?" Ford said.

"Hell, no, Jack," Wayne said. "You're the anchor—you'll bury us all."

"Oh, well," said Ford, "maybe I'll stick around a while longer then."

Like the old man in *The Quiet Man* who leaped from his deathbed at the prospect of a good fight, Ford seemed revived by Wayne's presence. They shared a drink or two and some memories. On Friday he didn't speak for a long while. Suddenly he said, "Would someone please get me a cigar," and they did. He didn't say anything more. Six hours later he was dead.

The *New York Times* obituary—like most obituaries anyway—emphasized all the wrong things, called him important for all the wrong reasons. Typically again, the man who had most vividly and memorably chronicled the American saga on the screen was more fittingly remembered in Europe. The major Italian papers gave his death more space than had either *The Times* of Los Angeles or New York. One headline called him "The creator of the Western," which, as such things go, was more accurate and appropriate than singling out *The Informer* as his masterpiece, as New York's paper of record had done. Italian and British TV featured several clips. In Yugoslavia, there was a two-hour television tribute. The funeral in Hollywood was well attended but, one heard, could well have used John Ford's touch. He knew how to bury the dead. There wasn't even a band to play "Shall We Gather at the River."

When Hawks went to see him that last Tuesday they talked for a couple of hours—mainly about a picture Hawks was planning. When he went out to speak to Mary, Ford's wife of 52 years, and Barbara, he told them, "Don't ever treat that man like a *mental* invalid—he just gave me some great ideas." Before leaving, Hawks went back to the bedroom.

"That you, Howard? I thought you left," said Ford, puffing on a cigar.

"Just came back to say goodbye, Jack."

"Goodbye, Howard."

Hawks started out of the room. "Howard," Ford called after him.

"Yes, Jack?"

"I mean *really* goodbye, Howard," he said.

"Really goodbye, Jack?"

"Really goodbye."

They shook hands, and Hawks left. As long as there are movies, how do you say goodbye to John Ford—rest, though I pray he does, in peace.

5 FORD'S CAREER

FILMOGRAPHY

(This filmography was compiled from several previously published ones augmented by a great deal of new information gathered from first-hand sources such as the collection of the Academy of Motion Pictures Arts and Sciences, and, particularly, the central files of Universal Studios.)

John Ford was born Sean Aloysius O'Feeney (the anglicized spelling of O'Fearna) on February 1, 1895 in Cape Elizabeth, Maine; he was the thirteenth (and last) child of Sean O'Feeney and the former Barbara Curran, who had come to America from Galway, Ireland. He died in Palm Desert, California on August 31, 1973. While he was still a baby, the family moved to Portland, Maine, where his father owned a saloon; summers were spent on Peak's Island (when he got older, he played a lot of 'summer baseball'). His father took him to Ireland several times, a sister 'came with us once,' he said. 'It was a very easy trip from Portland. We caught the boat right there and it landed in Galway, and then it was only a few miles over the hill to where my people lived.' "The Irish" was spoken around the house, and that's where he picked it up. 'Forgotten it all by now.'

After graduating from Portland High School in 1913, he came directly to Hollywood to get a job with his older (by thirteen years) brother, Francis, who had taken the name Ford and was a contract director-writer-actor at Universal Studios. Jack Ford (as he called himself) is listed in a 1916 issue of the *Motion Picture News* Studio Directory as an assistant director, but he says his screen career began as a laborer and then as a third assistant prop man.

1914 *Lucille Love—The Girl of Mystery* (Universal-Gold Seal).

Director: Francis Ford. Writer: 'The Master Pen' (pseudonym for F. Ford and Grace Cunard). Serial composed of 15 Chapters (2 reels each), one released every Tuesday beginning April 14. With Grace Cunard (Lucille Love), Francis Ford (Hugo Loubeque), Harry Rattenbury, Ernest Shields, E. M. Keller, Harry Schumm, Eddie Boland.

Universal's first serial, an international spy-chase-triangle melodrama, which Ford remembers having worked on as prop man. Probably he also played bits in the various chapters, did stunts (he often doubled his brother) and functioned as an all-around assistant.

1914 *Lucile, the Waitress* (Universal).
Director: Jack Ford. Author: Bide Dudley (from the New York Evening World.) A series of four two-reelers: 1) *She Wins a Prize and Has Her Troubles* (in which Lucile is given a winning raffle ticket, the prize for which turns out to be an ape—that gets loose; shooting March 7–17); 2) *Exaggeration Gets Her in All Kinds of Trouble* (in which a false rumor is spread that Lucile has inherited $500,000, and half the town chases after her; shooting March 19–April 3); 3) *She Gets Mixed Up in A Regular 'Kid Kalamity'* (in which she is baby-attendant at an annual convention, and causes chaos by mixing up the babies; shooting April 3–10); 4) *Her Near Proposal* (in which Lucile and her friends ransack the city dump in search of a letter from an old millionaire, thought to contain a marriage proposal; shooting April 20–28).

This series was found among the records at Universal, without cast lists or any information other than that printed above (and a complete synopsis of each story). No indication could be found there or elsewhere that any of these four shorts have ever been released.

Ford himself says he has no memory of them, and it *is* extremely early for him to have been directing (in fact, if it weren't for the start and completion dates, one would be sure they were unfilmed projects). However, there was a fire at Universal in 1914, and quite a few negatives were lost—perhaps this series was among them. (A couple of two-reelers based on the same characters were made at the studio in 1916.) Though they remain a mystery, we include them nevertheless, if for no other reason than as an example of the unbelievably poor state of film history and records (after all, it was only fifty years ago.)

The pictures that follow are probably only a sampling of the number Ford must have worked on between 1914 and 1917, when he started directing. Not only are the records incomplete, but he was often not billed as an actor, and it was not the custom to credit any behind-scene work other than directors, producers (in those days usually another word for directors), writers, and, rarely, photographers. However, it is a representative group and should give a fair idea of the kind of training he received. The vigor he was to bring to his pictures is reflected in the incredible energy required to work almost 52 weeks a year actually *making* movies.

1914 *The Mysterious Rose* (Universal-Gold Seal). Director: Francis Ford. Writer: Grace Cunard. Shooting: August 7–15. 2 reels. Released: November 24. With Francis Ford (Detective Phil Kelley), Grace Cunard (Lady Raffles), Jack Ford ('Bull' Feeney, her accomplice), Harry Schumm (the D.A.'s son), Wilbur Higby (The Ward Boss), Eddie Boland (Yeen Kee, Kelley's assistant).

One in 'a series of modern detective plays' (each featuring the wily Lady Raffles and Detective Kelley), which F. Ford and Cunard turned out intermittently through 1916.

1915 *The Birth of a Nation* (*The Clansman*) (Epoch Producing Corporation). Director-scenarist: D. W. Griffith. 12 reels. Released: February 8. Among the cast of thousands, as a member of the Ku Klux Klan: Jack Ford.

1915 *Three Bad Men and A Girl* (Universal-101 Bison). Director: Francis Ford. Writer: Grace Cunard. Shooting December 23–29, 1914. 2 reels. Released: February 20. With Francis Ford (Joe), Grace Cunard (the girl), Jack Ford (Jim), Major Paleologus (Shorty), Lewis Short (The Sheriff), F. J. Denecke (his assistant).

Three good men are mistaken for three bad men and jailed; freed eventually (without their guns), they capture the real outlaws bare-handed.

1915 *The Hidden City* (Universal-101 Bison). Director: Francis Ford. Writer: Grace Cunard. Shooting: January 23–February 8. 2 reels. Released: March 27. With Francis Ford (Lt. Johns), Jack Ford (his brother), Grace Cunard (Princess of the Hidden City), Eddie Polo (Poleau, her Minister).

A desert melodrama about a mythical underground city in India.

1915 *The Doorway of Destruction* (Universal-101 Bison). Director: Francis Ford. Writer: Grace Cunard. Assistant director: Jack Ford. Shooting February 26–March 4. 2 reels. Released: April 17. With Francis Ford (Col. Patrick Feeney), Jack Ford (his brother, Frank), Howard Daniels (his brother, Edward), Mina Cunard (Cecilia McLean, his sweetheart), Harry Schumm (Gen. McLean, her father).

When the Sepoy Rebellion breaks out, the British send the Irish Regiment on a suicide mission to break through the gates of a besieged city. Col. Feeney leads his men to victory (on the fourth assault) by waving the flag of Ireland. Placing the colors above the gates, he cries out to the British, 'March in ye dirty devils, the Irish Regiment has laid a carpet for you!' (Working title: *The Flag of Old Erin*.)

1915 *The Broken Coin* (Universal). Director: Francis Ford. Scenarist: Grace Cunard, from story by Emerson Hough. Assistant director: Jack Ford. Exteriors filmed in Bisbee, California. Serial composed of 22 Chapters (2 reels each), released weekly, beginning June 21. With Grace Cunard (Kitty Gray), Francis Ford (Count Frederick), Eddie Polo, Mina Cunard, Jack Ford, Harry Mann, Harry Schumm, Ernest Shields, Carl Laemmle (playing himself in the 1st and last episodes).

A search for the two halves of a coin which has on it the map to a priceless treasure.

1916 *The Lumber Yard Gang* (Universal-Rex). Director: Francis Ford. Writer: Grace Cunard. Shooting November 26–29, 1915. 933 feet. Released: February 15. With Francis Ford (Detective Phil Kelley), Elise Maison (Cecil McLean), Jack Ford (her brother, Head of the Lumber Yard Gang), William White (Chief of Detectives), Danny Bowen (Chief of Police).

A detective story, filled with 'hot' encounters between gangsters and police.

1916 *Chicken-Hearted Jim* (Universal-Rex). Director-writer: Francis Ford. Shooting November

10–17, 1915. 936 feet. Released: April 27. With Francis Ford (Jim Hardison), Mary Ford, Jo Ford (his sisters), John A. Ford (his father), Abbie Ford (his mother), Cecil McLean (Jib), Phil Kelley (her father), Pat Ford (The Mate), Jack Ford, Eddie Ford (the roughneck crew).

Jim is thought to be a coward, but during a mutiny, he proves his bravery. (Working title: *Chicken-Hearted Bill*.)

1916 *Peg O' The Ring* (Universal).
Directors: Francis Ford, Jacques Jaccard. Writer: Grace Cunard. Photographers: Harry Gant, Abel Vallet. Serial composed of 15 Chapters (2 reels each, except no. 1 which was 3), one released weekly beginning May 1. With Grace Cunard (Peg; Peg's mother), Francis Ford (Dr Lund, Jr.), Mark Fenton (Dr Lund, Sr.), Jack Ford (his accomplice), Pete Gerald (Flip), Jean Hathaway (Mrs Lund), Irving Lippner (Marcus, the Hindoo), Eddie Boland (his pal), Ruth Stonehouse, Charles Munn, G. Raymond Nye, Eddie Polo.

Melodrama set against a circus background, about a girl who is subject to strange spells because her mother had been clawed by a lion.

1916 *The Bandit's Wager* (Universal-Big U).
Director: Francis Ford. Writer: Grace Cunard. 1 reel. Released: November 5. With Francis Ford (The Bandit), Grace Cunard (Nan Jefferson), Jack Ford.

A westerner teaches his Eastern sister caution by pretending to be a notorious masked bandit.

It is possible that Jack Ford worked on some of the 16 chapters of Francis' 1916–17 serial *The Purple Mask*, though no evidence could be found to prove it.

1917 THE TORNADO (Universal-101 Bison).
Director-writer: Jack Ford. 2 reels. Released: March 3. With Jack Ford (Jack Dayton, 'No-gun man'), Jean Hathaway (his Irish mother), John Duffy (Slick, his partner), Pete Gerald (Pendleton, banker of Rock River), Elsie Thornton (his daughter Bess), Duke Worne (Lesparre, chief of the Cayote Gang).

Lesparre and his gang raid Rock River, rob the saloon and the bank, and kidnap Bess. Pendleton offers a $5,000 reward for her safe return, and Jack goes off unarmed to the rescue. (*Moving Picture World* (3/3/17): 'In his hand-to-hand struggle in the cabin and the jump from the cabin roof to the back of his horse, Jack Ford qualifies as a rough-riding expert . . . As a climax the hero leaps from his running horse onto a moving train!') He uses the reward money to bring his mother over from Ireland. *Ford*

remembers what was probably his first film as 'just a bunch of stunts.'

1917 *The Trail of Hate* (Universal-101 Bison).
Director-writer: Francis Ford. 2 reels. Released: April 28. With Jack Ford (the lieutenant), Louise Granville (the girl), Duke Worne (the captain), Jack Lawton.

This film is sometimes attributed to Jack, but according to *Motion Picture News* (4/28/17), it was directed by Francis; the plot has similarities to the latter's *Lucille Love* serial: A young Army lieutenant rescues a girl from outlaws and marries her; later, in the Philippines, she runs off with a captain who has always hated the lieutenant. When the two are captured by Moros, the lieutenant saves them both, but refuses to forgive the girl.

1917 THE SCRAPPER (Universal-101 Bison).
Director-writer: Jack Ford. Photographer: Ben Reynolds. 2 reels. Released: June 9. With Jack Ford (Buck, the scrapper), Louise Granville (Helen Dawson), Duke Worne (Jerry Martin, a parasite), Martha Hayes, Jean Hathaway.

Bored with the ranch, Buck's girl goes off to the city and gets involved (innocently) in a brothel. When Buck brings a herd of cattle to town, a streetwalker lures him to the house just in time for him to save his girl from Martin.

1917 THE SOUL HERDER (Universal-101 Bison).
Director: Jack Ford. Writer: George Hively. Photographer: Ben Reynolds. 3 reels. Released: August 7. With Harry Carey (Cheyenne Harry), Jean Hersholt (the Minister), Elizabeth James (his daughter), Molly Malone, Fritzi Ridgeway, Duke Lee, Vester Pegg, Bill Gettinger, Hoot Gibson.

Harry is thrown out of town and on his way across the desert meets a minister and his family; when the man is killed in an Indian raid, Harry takes care of his little daughter, later puts on the minister's frock, and reforms a town. *The first of Ford's 26 pictures with Harry Carey, and the one he himself likes to consider his first as a director. It was also Hoot Gibson's first appearance in a Ford film. Working title:* The Sky Pilot; *reissued as a two-reeler in 1922.*

1917 CHEYENNE'S PAL (Universal-Star Featurette).
Director: Jack Ford. Scenarist: Charles J. Wilson, Jr., from story by Ford. Photographer: Friend F. Baker. Shooting May 20–23. 2 reels. Released: August 13. With Harry Carey (Cheyenne Harry), Jim Corey (Noisy Jim), Gertrude Aster (dancehall girl), Vester

Pegg, Steve Pimento, Bill Gettinger, Hoot Gibson, Ed Jones (cowboys), Pete Carey (Cactus, the horse).

Very reluctantly, and only because he's broke, Harry sells his horse, Cactus, to an English quartermaster. When he overhears that the shipment of horses is being sent to France—probably to their death—he gets a job on the boat and that night jumps ship with Cactus. He is caught, but the captain lets Harry keep his horse and work off the money he owes. (Working titles: *Cactus My Pal, A Dumb Friend.*)

1917 STRAIGHT SHOOTING (Butterfly-Universal). Director: Jack Ford. Writer: George Hively. Photographer: George Scott. 5 reels. Released: August 27. With Harry Carey (Cheyenne Harry), Molly Malone (Joan Sims), Duke Lee ('Thunder' Flint), Vester Pegg ('Placer' Fremont), Hoot Gibson (Danny Morgan), George Berrell (Sweetwater Sims), Ted Brooks (Ted Sims), Milt Brown (Black-Eyed Pete).

Ford's first feature. Harry is hired by cattlemen to help them fight their war against the homesteaders, but he joins forces with the settlers when he finds out the cattlemen are terrorizing women and children. (Working titles: *The Cattle War, Joan of the Cattle Country;* re issued as a two-reeler, *Straight Shootin',* in January, 1925.)

1917 THE SECRET MAN (Butterfly-Universal). Director: Jack Ford. Writer: George Hively. Photographer: Ben Reynolds. 5 reels. Released: October 1. With Harry Carey (Cheyenne Harry), Morris Foster (Beauford), Elizabeth Jones (his child), Vester Pegg (Sheriff), Elizabeth Sterling (his sister, Molly), Bill Gettinger (foreman), Steve Clemente (Pedro, stage driver), Hoot Gibson.

The first part of the plot anticipates *Marked Men* (*Three Godfathers*): Fleeing the law, Harry finds his friend Beauford's little girl—who has survived a stagecoach accident but is dying of thirst—and takes her back to town though he knows he'll be caught as a result; there are other complications involving Beauford and Molly, who are secretly married, and Harry helps to clear them up. Moving Picture World (10/13/17): '. . . *a generous lot of picturesque scenes, flooded with California sunshine* . . .' (Working titles: *The Round Up, Up Against It.*)

1917 A MARKED MAN (Butterfly-Universal). Director: Jack Ford. Scenarist: George Hively, from story by Ford. Photographer: John W. Brown. 5 reels. Released: October 29. With Harry Carey (Cheyenne Harry), Molly Malone (Molly Young), Harry Rattenbury (her father, a rancher), Vester Pegg

(Kent), Mrs Townsend (Harry's mother), Bill Gettinger (sheriff), Hoot Gibson.

Kent lures Harry back to crime and together they pull a stage hold-up, during which Kent kills the driver. A posse catches them and as they're about to be hanged, a telegram arrives saying Harry's mother is coming for a visit; the sheriff allows him to pretend he's an honest citizen until she leaves. Back in jail again, Harry is reprieved when one of the stage passengers testifies it was Kent who fired the fatal shot. *Remade as Under Sentence (1920) by Ford's brother, Edward.*

1917 BUCKING BROADWAY (Butterfly-Universal). Director: Jack Ford. Producer: Harry Carey. Writer: George Hively. Photographer: John W. Brown. 5 reels. Released: December 24. With Harry Carey (Cheyenne Harry), Molly Malone (Helen Clayton), L. M. Wells (Ben Clayton, her father), Vester Pegg (Thornton, a cattle buyer).

Similar in plot to *The Scrapper*: Helen runs off with Thornton on the day her engagement to Harry was to have been announced. Following them to the city, and with the aid of a lady crook, Harry finds Helen, already disillusioned; his friends ride in to help him, and after a brawl along the rooftops, they win out over Thornton and his gang. '*Jack Ford again demonstrates his happy faculty for getting all outdoors into the scenes.*' (Moving Picture World, 12/22/17).

1918 THE PHANTOM RIDERS (Universal-Special). Director: Jack Ford. Producer: Harry Carey. Scenarist: George Hively, from story by Henry McRae. Photographer: John W. Brown. Shooting September 8–27, 1917. 5 reels. Released: January 28. With Harry Carey (Cheyenne Harry), Molly Malone (Molly) Buck Conners (her father), Vester Pegg (Leader of the 'Phantom Riders'), Bill Gettinger (Dave Bland), Jim Corey (foreman).

Bland has fenced off the Government grazing land called Paradise Creek, and with his 'unknown' masked riders he terrorizes any homesteader who questions his rights. Together with the Forest Rangers, Harry defeats Bland and wins Molly, whose father Bland murdered. (Working title: *The Range War.*)

1918 WILD WOMEN (Universal-Special). Director: Jack Ford. Producer: Harry Carey. Writer: George Hively. Photographer: John W. Brown. 5 reels. Released: February 25. With Harry Carey (Cheyenne Harry), Molly Malone (The Princess), Martha Maddox (The Queen), Vester Pegg, Ed Jones, E. Van Beaver, W. Taylor.

After winning the rodeo, Harry and his pals get drunk

on Honolulu cocktails and pass out. They are shanghaied, but when fire breaks out on the ship, they end up stranded on a South Seas Island, ruled over by a very possessive Queen. She takes a strong liking to Harry (anticipating perhaps the fat Indian girl's attachment to Jeff Hunter in *The Searchers*), but he much prefers the Princess, and *just* as he has won her love—he wakes up with a terrible hangover.

1918 THIEVES' GOLD (Universal-Special Feature). Director: Jack Ford. Scenarist: George Hively, from story, 'Back to the Right Trail,' by Frederick R. Bechdolt. Photographer: John W. Brown. 5 reels. Released: March 18. With Harry Carey (Cheyenne Harry), Molly Malone (Alice Norris), L. M. Wells (Savage), Vester Pegg (Simmons, an outlaw), John Cook (Larkin, stage driver), Harry Tenbrook, M. K. Wilson, Martha Maddox.

Restless, Harry leaves the Savage Ranch and falls in with Simmons. During their getaway after a gold robbery, Harry stops a runaway stagecoach, saves the passenger, Alice Norris, but is caught by the law. After Savage gets him released, Harry and Alice fall in love, but she finds out about his past and leaves him. In a showdown in the desert, Harry kills Simmons after being wounded, and it's Alice who finds him unconscious, saves his life and forgives him.

1918 THE SCARLET DROP (Universal-Special). Director: Jack Ford. Scenarist: George Hively, from story by Ford. Photographer: Ben Reynolds. 5 reels. Released: April 22. With Harry Carey ('Kaintuck' Harry Ridge), Molly Malone (Molly Calvert), Vester Pegg (Capt. Marley Calvert), M. K. Wilson (Graham Lyons), Betty Schade, Martha Maddox, Steve Clemente.

When Ft. Sumpter is fired upon, Kaintuck tries to join the Union Army, but Calvert rejects him as 'white trash.' Swearing vengeance, he joins Quantrill's Raiders, and when he comes upon Calvert's sister, Molly, he kidnaps her. But the two fall in love, and Kaintuck returns her to camp, where he is wounded defending her against Lyons (a blackmailer who found out her mother was Negro), whom he kills in the fight. Hearing the story, Calvert hides him in the attic, where his presence is betrayed to the officers hunting him by a drop of blood that leaks through the ceiling. Eventually he escapes back to Molly. (Working title: *Hill Billy*.)

1918 HELL BENT (Universal-Special Attraction). Director: Jack Ford. Writers: Ford, Harry Carey. Photographer: Ben Reynolds. 5,700 feet. Released:

June 29. With Harry Carey (Cheyenne Harry), Neva Gerber (Bess Thurston, his girl), Duke Lee (Cimarron Bill, his pal), Vester Pegg (Jack Thurston), Joseph Harris (Beau, an outlaw), M. K. Wilson, Steve Clemente.

Harry passes up a chance to capture Beau's outlaw gang because Bess's brother is one of them, but she mistakes his act for cowardice. Beau kidnaps Bess, and Harry tracks them to the desert where he and Beau shoot it out; both are wounded and all but one of their horses are killed. Harry sends Bess off for help and the two men set out on foot together. Beau dies during a sand storm, but Harry is rescued. '. . . few directors . . . put such sustained punch in their pictures as does this Mr Ford.' (Motion Picture News, 6/29/18).

1918 A WOMAN'S FOOL (Universal-Special Attraction). Director: Jack Ford. Scenarist: George Hively, from novel, *Lin McLean*, by Owen Wister. Photographer: Ben Reynolds. 60 minutes. Released: August 12. With Harry Carey (Lin McLean), Betty Schade (Katie), Roy Clark (Billy), Molly Malone (Jessie).

Katie, Lin's girl, runs off with a travelling salesman who turns out to be her husband. Lin finds her son, Billy, whom she deserted, adopts him, and eventually marries Jessie, the new station agent. After coming back and trying to wreck their marriage, Katie kills herself, and Billy brings Lin and Jessie back together.

1918 THREE MOUNTED MEN (Universal-Special Attraction). Director: Jack Ford. Writer: Eugene B. Lewis. Photographer: John W. Brown. 6 reels. Released: October 7. With Harry Carey (Cheyenne Harry), Joe Harris (Buck Masters), Neva Gerber (Lola Masters), Harry Carter (the warden's son), Mrs. Anna Townsend.

The warden's son is being black-mailed by Buck Masters and promises Harry a pardon if he can get Masters arrested again. On the outside, Harry hears of Buck's plan to rob a stage, alerts the law, and Masters is caught. But when he discovers that his girl friend Lola is Buck's sister, Harry and his brothers ride after the posse and help Masters to escape.

Some filmographies erroneously list Jack Ford in the cast of Francis Ford's 1918–19 serial, *The Silent Mystery*, and also as co-director of *The Craving* (1919; working title, *Delirium*). 'That was made by my brother Francis,' Ford says about the latter, and Universal's records bear him out.

1919 ROPED (Universal-Special). Director: Jack Ford. Writer: Eugene B. Lewis.

Photographer: John W. Brown. 6 reels. Released: January 13. With Harry Carey (Cheyenne Harry), Neva Gerber (Aileen Judson Brown), Molly McConnell (Mrs Judson Brown), J. Farrell McDonald (butler), Arthur Shirley (Ferdie Van Duzen).

As a joke, Harry's cowhands place an advertisement in an Eastern paper asking for a wife for their boss. Mrs Brown, a bankrupt society woman, forces her daughter Aileen to answer it, but when Harry comes East—the two fall in love and marry. Harry isn't very successful in society, and besides Mrs Brown would much prefer to be getting alimony cheques, so after Aileen has a child, Mrs Brown manages to break up the marriage. Back at the ranch again, Harry gets a wire from the butler telling him to come back and take a look around, which he does—along with his cowboys— and they straighten things out. *The first appearance of J. Farrell McDonald in a Ford film; he was to act in over twenty others.*

1919 THE FIGHTING BROTHERS (Universal).
Director: Jack Ford. Scenarist: George Hively, from story by George C. Hull. Photographer: John W. Brown. Shooting February 8–15. 2 reels. Released: March 10. With Pete Morrison (Sheriff Pete Larkin), Hoot Gibson (Lonnie Larkin), Yvette Mitchell (Conchita), Jack Woods (Ben Crawley), Duke Lee (Slim).

When Sheriff Larkin's brother is falsely accused of a murder, Larkin still does his job—arrests the boy and takes him to prison. But, his duty done, the sheriff takes off his badge and helps his brother to escape. (Working title: *His Buddy*.)

1919 A FIGHT FOR LOVE (Universal-Special Attraction).
Director: Jack Ford. Writer: Eugene B. Lewis. Photographer: John W. Brown. Exteriors filmed in California's Big Bear region. 6 reels. Released: March 24. With Harry Carey (Cheyenne Harry), Joe Harris (Black Michael), Neva Gerber (Kate McDougal), Mark Fenton (Angus McDougal, her father), J. Farrell McDonald (The Priest), Princess Neola Mae (Little Fawn), Chief Big Tree (Swift Deer).

The Northwest Mounties are after Harry for the murder of an Indian boy, and the only witness to the crime is a Priest—who can't tell what he saw because the real killer, Black Michael, has confessed to him. When Michael kidnaps Kate, Harry follows them to a river hide-out, and in the ensuing struggle, Michael falls over a cliff. Dying, he confesses once more—but this time to the law. (Working title: *Hell's Neck*.)

1919 BY INDIAN POST (Universal).
Director: Jack Ford. Scenarist: H. Tipton Steck

from story, 'The Trail of the Billy-Doo,' by William Wallace Cook. Shooting began February 18. 2 reels. Released: April 12. With Pete Morrison (Jode McWilliams), Duke Lee (Pa Owens), Magda Lane (Peg Owens), Ed Jones (Stumpy, the cook), Jack Woods (Dutch), Harley Chambers (Fritz), Hoot Gibson (Chub), Jack Walters (Andy), Otto Myers (Swede), Jim Moore (Two-Horns, an Indian).

Jode loves Peg so he gets Stumpy to write a love letter for him, which Stumpy does—copying it from 'Lothario's Compendium.' While Jode is asleep, the other cowboys find the letter and tack it to the bunkhouse door where Two-Horns finds it. Admiring the 'paper-talk,' he takes it down to show everyone he meets. Jode rides off to stop him, but before he can, the letter gets to Peg—and has the intended effect. (Working title: *The Love Letter*.)

1919 THE RUSTLERS (Universal).
Director: Jack Ford. Writer: George Hively. Photographer: John W. Brown. Shooting February 28– March 8. 2 reels. Released: April 26. With Pete Morrison (Ben Clayburn), Helen Gibson (Postmistress Nell Wyndham), Jack Woods (Sheriff Buck Farley), Hoot Gibson (his deputy).

Disguised as a peaceful sheepman, Clayburn is actually a Government Ranger sent to Point Rock to find the leaders of a band of rustlers. When he is himself accused of being one of them, Nell saves him from a lynch mob and together they round up the real outlaws. (Working title: *Even Money*.)

1919 BARE FISTS (Universal-Special).
Director: Jack Ford. Scenarist: Eugene B. Lewis, from story by Bernard McConville. Photographer: John W. Brown. Shooting began July 20, 1918. 5,500 feet. Released: May 5. With Harry Carey (Cheyenne Harry), Molly McConnell (his mother) Joseph Girard (his father), Howard Ensteadt (his brother, Bud), Betty Schade (Conchita), Vester Pegg (Lopez), Joe Harris (Boone Travis), Anna Mae Walthall (Ruby, a dance hall girl).

Harry's father is killed in a gunfight, and his mother makes him swear he'll never again use his gun, and rely only on his bare fists. But when his little brother is branded on the chest by cattle rustlers, Harry breaks his promise. (Working title: *The Man Who Wouldn't Shoot*.)

1919 GUN LAW (Universal).
Director: Jack Ford. Writer: H. Tipton Steck. Photographer: John W. Brown. Shooting March 11– 21. 2 reels. Released: May 10. With Pete Morrison (Dick Allen), Hoot Gibson (Bart Stevens, alias Smoke

Gublen), Helen Gibson (Letty), Jack Woods (Cayuse Yates), Otto Myers, Ed Jones, H. Chambers (Yates' gang).

Secret Serviceman Allen takes a job at Bart Stevens' mine in order to find evidence proving that Stevens is a mail robber called Smoke Gublen. He does—but by then he is in love with the man's sister—and to make things harder, Stevens saves his life. The recovery of the untouched mail bags eases his decision. (Working title: *The Posse's Prey.*)

1919 THE GUN PACKER (Universal).
Director: Jack Ford. Scenarist: Karl R. Coolidge, from story by Ford and Harry Corley. Photographer: John W. Brown. Shooting began March 25. 2 reels. Released: May 24. With Ed Jones (Sandy McLoughlin), Pete Morrison ('Pearl Handle' Wiley), Magda Lane (Rose McLoughlin), Jack Woods (Pecos Smith), Hoot Gibson (outlaw leader), Jack Walters (Brown), Duke Lee (Buck Landers), Howard Enstedt (Bobby McLoughlin).

With the help of a reformed gunman (and a gang of outlaws recruited as a final recourse), the sheepmen win their water rights from the cattle barons of Rimrock Valley. (Working title: *Out Wyoming Way;* reissued in August, 1924.)

1919 RIDERS OF VENGEANCE (Universal-Special).
Director: Jack Ford. Producer: P. A. Powers. Writers: Ford, Harry Carey. Photographer: John W. Brown. 6 reels. Released: June 9. With Harry Carey (Cheyenne Harry), Seena Owen (the Girl), Joe Harris (Sheriff Gale Thurston), J. Farrell McDonald (Buell), Jennie Lee (Harry's mother), Glita Lee (Virginia), Alfred Allen, Betty Schade, Vester Pegg, M. K. Wilson.

Harry's family has a lot of enemies in Mesquite, and on his wedding day, as he and his new wife are coming out of church, the bride is murdered. Harry disappears, but two years later he returns to post the names of the men he plans to murder in revenge. After killing the first, he meets Thurston's girl (Harry believes Thurston was the leader of the gang that killed his wife), and considers harming her, but can't; he falls in love with her. Later, Harry and Thurston are trapped by Apaches and he discovers the man is innocent; he tries desperately to save him for the girl they both love, but Thurston dies.

1919 THE LAST OUTLAW (Universal).
Director: Jack Ford. Scenarist: H. Tipton Steck, from story by Evelyne Murray Campbell. Photographer: John W. Brown. Shooting April 8–12. 2 reels. Released: June 14. With Ed 'King Fisher'

Jones (Bud Coburn), Richard Cumming (Sheriff Brownlo), Lucille Hutton (Idaleen Coburn), Jack Walters (Chad Allen), Billie Hutton.

After ten years in jail, Bud comes back home to find the town gone 'civilized and dry,' and his daughter running around with a bootlegger who plans to take her away—but not as his wife. The old outlaw has to kidnap his daughter and get wounded before he can save her from herself. (Reissued in December, 1923; remade as a feature in 1936.)

1919 THE OUTCASTS OF POKER FLAT (Universal-Special).
Director: Jack Ford. Producer: P. A. Powers. Scenarist: H. Tipton Steck, from stories, 'The Outcasts of Poker Flat' and 'The Luck of Roaring Camp,' by Bret Harte. Photographer: John W. Brown. 6 reels. Released: July 6. With Harry Carey (Square Shootin' Lanyon; John Oakhurst), Cullen Landis (Billy Lanyon; Tommy Oakhurst), Gloria Hope (Ruth Watson; Sophy), J. Farrell McDonald, Charles H. Mailes, Victor Potel, Joe Harris, Duke R. Lee, Vester Pegg.

The story is framed with a prologue and epilogue in which Carey reads the Harte book to his son: John Oakhurst, 'the honest gambler,' is lonely, so he adopts an infant boy, who, when he grows up, falls in love with the same girl Oakhurst loves. The gambler gives her up for his adopted son. Photoplay: '. . . *marvelous river locations and absolutely incomparable photography . . .' Remakes in 1937 and in 1952, directed, respectively, by Christy Cabanne and Joseph M. Newman.*

1919 THE ACE OF THE SADDLE (Universal-Special). Director: Jack Ford. Producer: P. A. Powers. Scenarist: George Hively, from story by B. J. Jackson. Photographer: John W. Brown. Exteriors filmed in the Rio Grande Valley. 6 reels. Released: August 18. With Harry Carey (Cheyenne Harry Henderson), Joe Harris (Sheriff 'Two-Gun' Hildebrand of Yucca County), Duke R. Lee (Sheriff Faulkner of Pinkerton County), Peggy Pearce (Madeline Faulkner, his daughter), Jack Walters (Inky O'Day), Vester Pegg (gambler), Zoe Ray, Howard Enstedt (the children), Ed 'King Fisher' Jones ('Home Sweet' Holmes), William Cartwright ('Humpy' Anderson).

Harry goes to Pinkerton county (to get help against Yucca's crooked judge and sheriff) and falls in love with Madeline, who makes him promise to give up his guns. So at the end, after he and his pals rope his cabin and drag it over the county line, Harry fends off the night riders by throwing lighted sticks of dynamite at them. (Working title: *A Man of Peace.*)

1919 THE RIDER OF THE LAW (Universal-Special). Director: Jack Ford. Producer: P. A. Powers

Scenarist: H. Tipton Steck, from story, 'Jim of the Rangers,' by G. P. Lancaster. Photographer: John W. Brown. 5 reels. Released: November 3. With Harry Carey (Jim Kyneton), Gloria Hope (Betty, his girl), Vester Pegg (Nick Kyneton), Theodore Brooks (The Kid), Joe Harris (Buck Soutar), Jack Woods (Jack West), Duke R. Lee (Capt. Graham Saltire), Claire Anderson (Roseen), Jennie Lee (mother).

Texas Ranger Jim Kyneton has to arrest his foster brother, Nick, and his friends, but they escape with the help of Roseen, a girl Jim once rejected. The Ranger catches all of them except Nick, who kills himself rather than face the shame. Exhibitors Trade Review: '. . . chases, flying bullets, falling men, both good and bad, both sorts of women and a lot of scenery . . .'

1919 A GUN FIGHTIN' GENTLEMAN (Universal-Special).

Director: Jack Ford. Producer: P. A. Powers. Scenarist: Hal Hoadley, from story by Ford and Harry Carey. Photographer: John W. Brown. 5 reels. Released: November 30. With Harry Carey (Cheyenne Harry), J. Barney Sherry (John Merritt), Kathleen O'Conner (Helen Merritt), Lydia Yeamans Titus (her aunt), Harry von Meter (Earl of Jollywell), Duke R. Lee (Buck Regan), Joe Harris (Seymour), Johnny Cooke (the old sheriff), Ted Brooks (the 'Youngster').

Harry goes to Chicago to stop meat packer-cattle king John Merritt from stealing his property, but Merritt's family laughs at his crude manners, and refuses to listen to his case. He steals the Merritt pay-roll and then returns it, but that doesn't get him anywhere—so he steals Merritt's daughter, and they fall in love. Exhibitors Trade Review: '. . . the kind of picture that Harry Carey and Jack Ford can do better together than any other actor and director in the world.'

1919 MARKED MEN (Universal-Special).

Director: Jack Ford. Producer: P. A. Powers. Scenarist: H. Tipton Steck, from story, 'The Three Godfathers,' by Peter B. Kyne. Photographer: John W. Brown. Editors: Frank Lawrence, Frank Atkinson. 5 reels. Released: December 21. With Harry Carey (Cheyenne Harry), J. Farrell McDonald (Tom 'Placer' McGraw), Joe Harris (Tom Gibbons), Winifred Westover (Ruby Merrill), Ted Brooks (Tony Garcia), Charles Lemoyne (Sheriff Pete Cushing), David Kirby (Warden 'Bruiser' Kelly).

Harry and his two friends break jail, separate and meet again in a mining camp; his friends talk him into another bank robbery and this time they are chased out into the Mojave Desert, where they come upon a dying mother and her baby. The three decide to give up their

120

freedom in order to save the child, but only one of them survives the journey. Ford's favourite among his early films. The first version of this story was made in 1916 as a feature called The Three Godfathers, also starring Harry Carey, and directed by Edward J. LeSaint. Subsequently, it was made in 1929 (Hell's Heroes, directed by William Wyler), 1936 (Three Godfathers, directed by Richard Boleslawski), and 1948 (Ford's own remake). Working title: The Trail of Shadows.

1920 THE PRINCE OF AVENUE A (Universal-Special).

Director: Jack Ford. Scenarist: Charles J. Wilson, Jr., from story by Charles and Frank Dazey. Photographer: John W. Brown. 5 reels. Released: February 23. With James J. 'Gentleman Jim' Corbett (Barry O'Conner), Mary Warren (Mary Tompkins), Harry Northrup (Edgar Jones), Cora Drew (Mary O'Conner), Richard Cummings (Patrick O'Conner), Frederik Vroom (William Tompkins), Mark Fenton (Father O'Toole), George Vanderlip (Reggie Vanderlip), Johnny Cooke (butler), Lydia Yeamans Titus (housekeeper), George Fisher.

Ford's first non-western: Boss Patrick O'Conner wants William Tompkins as candidate for mayor; but when O'Conner's son, Barry, is thrown out of the Tompkins house for boorish behaviour towards their daughter, Mary, O'Conner gets furious. Tompkins becomes worried about his political future, so he and Mary go to O'Conner's house to apologize and she consents to be Barry's partner at the Grand Ball. There, Edgar Jones, O'Conner's arch political rival, insults her, but Barry takes on Jones and his crowd, polishes them off, saves the day and wins the girl.

1920 THE GIRL IN No. 29 (Universal-Special).

Director: Jack Ford. Scenarist: Philip J. Hurn, from story, 'The Girl in the Mirror,' by Elizabeth Jordan. Photographer: John W. Brown. 5 reels. Released: April 3. With Frank Mayo (Laurie Devon), Harry Hilliard (Rodney Bangs), Claire Anderson (Doris Williams), Elinor Fair (Barbara Devon), Bull Montana (Abdullah the Strangler), Ray Ripley (Ransome Shaw), Robert Bolder (Jacob Epstein).

Devon has written one hit play but can't seem to get back to work. Through his window one day, he sees a girl in the apartment across the street putting a revolver to her head—he reaches her just in time. When she is kidnapped to a Long Island mansion, Devon gives chase and rescues her, killing one of the criminals. While he is recounting the adventure to his friends, the man he shot walks into the room: Devon's sister and friends staged the whole thing. Finally he has something to write about, and the new play becomes a hit. This plot bears a strong resemblance to Allan Dwan's Manhattan Madness (1916), which, in turn, was no doubt inspired by the successful play and novel, Seven Keys to Baldpate (film versions in 1917, 1925, 1930, 1935, 1947).

1920 HITCHIN' POSTS (Universal-Special). Director: Jack Ford. Scenarist: George C. Hull, from story by Harold M. Schumate. Photographer: Benjamin Kline. 5 reels. Released: August 29. With Frank Mayo (Jefferson Todd), Beatrice Burnham (Ophelia Bereton), Joe Harris (Raoul Castiga), J. Farrell McDonald (Joe Alabam), Mark Fenton (Col. Carl Bereton), Dagmar Godowsky (Octoroon), Duke R. Lee (Col. Lancy), C. E. Anderson (steamboat captain), M. Biddulph (Maj. Gray).

The Civil War turns a Southern gentleman named Todd into a Mississippi riverboat gambler. When he wins Col. Bereton's last possession—his four prized race horses—the colonel commits suicide, leaving a penniless daughter. Feeling responsible for her father's death, Todd takes her into his care and, later, against the background of a land rush, he saves her from a badman. *Very similar in plot to the Booth Tarkington-Henry Leon Wilson play*, Cameo Kirby, *which had already been made into a film in 1914 (supervised by Cecil B. DeMille), and which Ford himself was to remake in 1923.*

Ford has no memory of having worked in any capacity on his brother Francis' 1920 serial, The Mystery of 13, nor of having shot footage ('I *know* I didn't') for the Maurice Tourneur production, The Great Redeemer, made the same year; both films are tentatively listed in at least one Ford filmography, but no other evidence can be found to support these credits.

1920 *Under Sentence* (Universal). Director: Edward Feeney. Scenarist: George Hively, from story by Jack Ford. Shooting started April 12. 2 reels. Released: June 12. With Bob Anderson, Ethel Ritchie, Jennie Lee, J. Farrell McDonald, Cap Anderson, Jack Woods.

A remake of Ford's 1917 feature, A Marked Man, directed by Jack's brother, who later was to spell his name O'Fearna and work as an assistant director on many of Ford's pictures.

On July 3, 1920, Ford married Mary McBryde Smith.

1920 JUST PALS (Fox-20th Century Brand). Director: Jack Ford. Scenarist: Paul Schofield, from story by John McDermott. Photographer: George Schneiderman. 5 reels. Released: November 14.

With Buck Jones (Bim), Helen Ferguson (Mary Bruce, the school teacher), George E. Stone (Bill), Duke R. Lee (sheriff), William Buckley (Harvey Cahill), Edwin Booth Tilton (Dr Stone), Eunice Murdock Moore (Mrs Stone), Burt Apling (brakeman), Slim Padgett, Pedro Leone (outlaws), Ida Tenbrook (maid), John J. Cooke (elder).

The story of the town loafer ('just *watching* people work makes Bim tired') and how his friendship with a 13-year-old boy (who jumped off the train going through town) changes him. *Ford's first film away from Universal:* 'Buck Jones was very good—that's when they suddenly discovered Buck was an actor.' (George Schneiderman's first picture with Ford.)

1921 THE BIG PUNCH (Fox-20th Century Brand). Director: Jack Ford. Scenarists: Ford, Jules Furthman, from story Fighting Back by Furthman. Photographer: Jack B. Good. 5 reels. Released: January 30. With Buck Jones (Buck), Barbara Bedford (Hope Standish), George Siegmann (Flash McGraw), Jack Curtis (Jed, Buck's brother), Jack McDonald, Al Fremont (Jed's friends), Edgar Jones (sheriff), Irene Hunt (dance hall girl), Eleanor Gilmore (Salvation Army girl).

Sent to prison on a bum rap, Buck is involved in a daring jail break. Free again, he rescues a Salvation Army girl from a lecherous saloon owner, becomes a minister in her Army and reforms the scoffing town.

1921 THE FREEZE OUT (Universal-Special). Director: Jack Ford. Writer: George C. Hull. Photographer: Harry C. Fowler. 4,400 feet. Released: April 9. With Harry Carey (Ohio, The Stranger), Helen Ferguson (Zoe Whipple), Joe Harris (Headlight Whipple), Charles Lemoyne (Denver Red), J. Farrell McDonald (Bobtail McGuire), Lydia Yeamans Titus (Mrs McGuire).

When The Stranger finds the town's only gambling hall to be crooked, he decides to open his own. Zoe talks to him about reforming the vice-ridden community, and, though he pretends to ignore her, his gambling hall opens as a school for the children.

1921 THE WALLOP (Universal-Special). Director: Jack Ford. Scenarist: George C. Hull, from story, 'The Girl He Left Behind Him,' by Eugene Manlove Rhodes. Photographer: Harry C. Fowler. 5 reels. Released: May 7. With Harry Carey (John Wesley Pringle), Joe Harris (Barela), Charles Lemoyne (Matt Lisner), J. Farrell McDonald (Neuces River), Mignonne Golden (Stella Vorhis), Bill Gettinger (Christopher Foy), Noble Johnson (Espinol), C. E. Anderson (Applegate), Mark Fenton (Major Vorhis).

While watching a 'Handsome Harry' movie, Pringle recognizes an old girlfriend sitting next to him. (The picture is so bad they walk out.) He realizes that he still loves her, but the girl loves someone else—a young man who gets in trouble with a crooked sheriff and hides in the mountains. Pringle rides out and captures the youth 'for the reward,' but then helps him escape from the sheriff so that the boy can return to the girl they both love. (Working title: *The Homeward Trail*.)

1921 DESPERATE TRAILS (Universal-Special).

Director: Jack Ford. Scenarist: Elliott J. Clawson, from story, 'Christmas Eve at Pilot Butte,' by Courtney Riley Cooper. Photographers: Harry C. Fowler, Robert DeGrasse. Shooting March 14–April 11. 5 reels. Released: July 9. With Harry Carey (Bart Carson), Irene Rich (Mrs Walker), George E. Stone (Danny Boy), Helen Field (Carrie), Barbara La Marr (Lady Lou), George Siegmann (Sheriff Price), Charles Insley (Dr Higgins), Ed Coxen (Walter A. Walker).

When Carson's girlfriend leaves him, he turns to the Widow Walker, realizing that he had always loved her; he even goes to jail for something he didn't do just to protect *her* brother. But in prison, he finds out the truth: Walter was *not* her brother, he was her husband. On Christmas Eve he escapes from jail to track the man down. Motion Picture News *wrote*: '. . . *the closing reels show the slow change of seasons in the trackless forest, another nice piece of camera work and direction.' Ford remembers the film with affection (under its working title,* Christmas Eve at Pilot Butte), *because his son, Patrick Roper, was born during the shooting (on April 3). It was also the first time he had worked to such an extent with night time photography, and, he feels, it turned out well. On several occasions he has spoken of wanting to remake the picture.*

1921 ACTION (Universal-Special).

Director: Jack Ford. Scenarist: Harvey Gates, from "The Mascotte of the Three Star" by J. Allan Dunn. Photographer: John W. Brown. 5 reels. Released: September 12. With Hoot Gibson (Sandy Brooke), Francis Ford (Soda Water Manning), J. Farrell McDonald (Mormon Peters), Buck Conners (Pat Casey), Byron Munson (Henry Meekin), Clara Horton (Molly Casey), William R. Daly (J. Plimsoll), Charles Newton (Sheriff Dipple), Jim Corey (Sam Waters), Ed 'King Fisher' Jones (Art Smith), Dorothea Wolburt (Mirandy Meekin).

When Molly's father is killed, three desert bums buy her ranch, and some local outlaws figure there must be gold on the land. They try to steal it through guardianship of the girl, who's under-age, so the bums send her off to an Eastern boarding school. Much to their

surprise, they discover there *is* gold on the land, Molly returns, and she and Sandy fall in love. *Francis Ford's first appearance in a film of his brother's. Working title:* Let's Go.

1921 SURE FIRE (Universal-Special).

Director: Jack Ford. Scenarist: George C. Hull, from story, 'Bransford of Rainbow Ridge,' by Eugene Manlove Rhodes. Photographer: Virgil G. Miller. 5 reels. Released: November 5. With Hoot Gibson (Jeff Bransford), Molly Malone (Marian Hoffman), Reeves 'Breezy' Eason, Jr. (Sonny), Harry Carter (Rufus Coulter), Murdock MacQuarrie (Major Parker), Fritzi Brunette (Elinor Parker), George Fisher (Burt Rawlings), Charles Newton (Leo Ballinger), Jack Woods (Brazos Bart), Jack Walters (Overland Kid), Joe Harris (Romero), Steve Clemente (Gomez), Mary Philbin.

A wife's lover steals the husband's money. By accident, Jeff is coming out of the house just as the husband returns to discover the theft, and thinking him the robber, he starts after Jeff. In the meantime, bandits kill the lover and *they* steal the money. Finally, Jeff, who can't pay his mortgage because he's too busy running from the husband, catches the bandits, returns the money, pays his mortgage, and gets the girl. The husband never does find out about the lover.

For the next ten years, Ford was to work exclusively for Fox.

1921 JACKIE (Fox).

Director: Jack Ford. Scenarist: Dorothy Yost, from story by Countess Helena Barcynska (pseudonym for Marguerite Florence Helene Jervis Evans). Photographer: George Schneiderman. 5 reels. Released: November 27. With Shirley Mason (Jackie), William Scott (Mervyn Carter), Harry Carter (Bill Bowman), George E. Stone (Benny), Elsie Bambrick (Millie), John Cooke (Winter).

Jackie, a Russian girl in a cheap roadshow, wants to be a great dancer and, to escape a lustful theatre manager, she flees to London, where a young American helps her realize her ambition.

1922 LITTLE MISS SMILES (Fox).

Director: Jack Ford. Scenarist: Dorothy Yost, from *Little Aliens* by Myra Kelly, adapted by Yost and Jack Strumwasser. Photographer: David Abel. 5 reels. Released: January 15. With Shirley Mason (Esther Aaronson), Gaston Glass (Dr. Jack Washton), George Williams (Papa Aaronson), Martha Franklin (Mama Aaronson), Arthur Rankin (Davie Aaronson), Baby Blumfield (Baby Aaronson), Richard Lapan (Leon

Aaronson), Alfred Testa (Louis Aaronson), Sidney D'Albrook ('The Spider').

The story of a Jewish family in New York's ghetto: about the mother's failing eyesight (which is restored), the daughter's love for the doctor (which is returned), and her brother's involvement in a murder (of which he is cleared).

1922 *Silver Wings* (Fox).
Directors: Edwin Carewe (The Play), Jack Ford (The Prologue). Writer: Paul H. Sloane. Photographers: Joseph Ruttenberg, Robert Kurrle. 8,271 feet. Released: August 27. With (in the Prologue): Mary Carr (Anna Webb), Lynn Hammond (John Webb), Knox Kincaid (John, their child), Joseph Monahan (Harry, another son), Maybeth Carr (Ruth, their daughter), Claude Brook (Uncle Andrews), Robert Hazelton (The Priest), Florence Short (Widow), May Kaiser (baby); *and* (in The Play): Mary Carr (Anna Webb), Percy Helton (John), Joseph Striker (Harry), Jane Thomas (Ruth), Roy Gordon (George), Florence Haas (Little Anna), Claude Brook (Uncle Andrews), Roger Lytton (banker), Ernest Hilliard (Jerry).

John Webb invents a sewing machine and his family becomes rich. After his death, Anna puts her sons in charge of the business and her eldest runs it into debt, reducing them to poverty again, and the family breaks up; eventually they are re-united. *Ford's 'Prologue' dealt only with the family's very early life.*

1922 THE VILLAGE BLACKSMITH (Fox).
Director: Jack Ford. Scenarist: Paul H. Sloane, from poem by Henry Wadsworth Longfellow. Photographer: George Schneiderman. 8 reels. Released: November 2. With William Walling (John Hammond, blacksmith), Virginia True Boardman (his wife), Virginia Valli (Alice Hammond), David Butler (Bill Hammond), Gordon Griffith (Bill, as child), Ida Nan McKenzie (Alice, as child), George Hackthorne (Johnnie), Pat Moore (Johnnie, as child), Tully Marshall (Squire Ezra Brigham), Caroline Rankin (Mrs Brigham), Ralph Yeardsley (Anson Brigham), Henri de la Garrique (Anson, as child), Francis Ford (Asa Martin), Bessie Love (Rosemary Martin), Helen Field (Rosemary, as child), Mark Fenton (Dr Brewster), Lon Poff (Gideon Crane, school teacher), Cordelia Callahan (Aunt Hattie), Eddie Gribbon (village gossip), Lucile Hutton (flapper).

The idyllic early American life of a blacksmith and his family is disrupted—for a time—by a scandal that's based on lies.

On December 16, 1922, the Fords had a daughter, Barbara Nugent.

1923 THE FACE ON THE BARROOM FLOOR (Fox).
Director: Jack Ford. Scenarists: Eugene B. Lewis, G. Marion Burton, from poem by Hugh Antoine D'Arcy. Photographer: George Schneiderman. 5,787 feet. Released: January 1. With Henry B. Walthall (Robert Stevens, an artist), Ruth Clifford (Marion Von Vleck), Walter Emerson (Richard Von Vleck), Alma Bennett (Lottie), Norval McGregor (Governor), Michael Dark (Henry Drew), Gus Saville (fisherman).

An artist tells his story to some workers in a bar: about the girl he lost through a misunderstanding, his degradation and time in prison on a false charge, his final reprieve through an act of bravery. 'The Face on the Barroom Floor!' Ford once said, 'My God, did I do *that ?'* (*In 1914, Chaplin had done a parody of the poem, under the same title.*)

1923 THREE JUMPS AHEAD (Fox).
Director-writer: Jack Ford. Photographer: Daniel B. Clark. 4,854 feet. Released: March 25. With Tom Mix (Steve Clancy), Alma Bennett (Annie Darrell), Virginia True Boardman (Mrs Darrell), Edward Piel (Taggitt), Joe E. Girard (Annie's father), Francis Ford (Virgil), Margaret Joslin (Juliet), Henry Todd (Cicero), Buster Gardner (Brutus).

A band of outlaws captures Clancy and his uncle and holds them in a cave, where another prisoner is forced to flog them. When this old man escapes, Clancy is told to get him back or they'll kill his uncle. Through a trick, Clancy finally manages to recapture the man—only to find he has to rescue him again—because he has fallen in love with the old guy's daughter.

1923 CAMEO KIRBY (Fox).
Director: John Ford. Scenarist: Robert N. Lee, from play by Harry Leon Wilson and Booth Tarkington. Photographer: George Schneiderman. 7 reels. Released (with tinted sequences): October 21. With John Gilbert (Cameo Kirby), Gertrude Olmstead (Adele Randall), Alan Hale (Colonel Moreau), William E. Lawrence (Colonel Randall), Jean Arthur (Ann Playdell), Richard Tucker (Cousin Aaron), Phillips Smalley (Judge Playdell), Jack McDonald (Larkin Bruce), Eugenie Ford (Mme. Dauezac).
Kirby joins a dishonest card game just to help an old man who is being fleeced; he wins everything, planning to return it, but the old man doesn't know his intentions and commits suicide. His daughter is the girl Kirby loves and by the end, she comes to realize Cameo's true character. Moving Picture World (10/27/23): *'Director John Ford [this was the first film on which he was billed John instead of Jack] has been especially skilful in framing each scene to artistic advantage. . . .'*

(*Remade in* 1929 *by Irving Cummings.*)

1923 NORTH OF HUDSON BAY (Fox).

Director: John Ford. Writer: Jules Furthman. Photographer: Daniel B. Clark. 4,973 feet. Released (with tinted sequences): November 19. With Tom Mix (Michael Dane, a rancher), Kathleen Key (Estelle MacDonald), Jennie Lee (Dane's mother), Frank Campeau (Cameron MacDonald), Eugene Pallette (Peter Dane), Will Walling (Angus MacKenzie), Frank Leigh (Jeffry Clough), Fred Kohler (Armand LeMoir).

On a steamboat heading North, where his brother has struck gold, Mike Dane falls in love with Estelle MacDonald. When he arrives at the Canadian trading post, Dane learns that his brother has been murdered and his partner sentenced to death as the killer. But Estelle's uncle turns out to be the real murderer and during a chase he is accidentally killed. (Working title: *Journey of Death.*)

1923 HOODMAN BLIND (Fox).

Director: John Ford. Scenarist: Charles Kenyon, from play by Henry Arthur Jones and Wilson Barrett. Photographer: George Schneiderman. 5,434 feet. Released: December 20. With David Butler (Jack Yeulette), Gladys Hulette (Nance Yeulette; Jessie Walton), Regina Connelly (Jessie Walton, the 1st), Frank Campeau (Mark Lezzard), Marc MacDermott (John Linden), Trilby Clark (Mrs. John Linden), Eddie Gribbon (Battling Brown), Jack Walters (Bull Yeaman).

A fisherman who deserted two families, returns after twenty years (a wealthy man now) to try and make up for his past sins.

1924 THE IRON HORSE (Fox).

Director: John Ford. Scenarist: Charles Kenyon, from story by Kenyon and John Russell. Photographers: George Schneiderman, Burnett Guffey. Titles: Charles Darnton. Music score: Erno Rapee. Assistant director: Edward O'Fearna. 11,335 feet. Released (with tinted sequences): August 28. With George O'Brien (Davy Brandon), Madge Bellamy (Miriam Marsh), Judge Charles Edward Bull (Abraham Lincoln), William Walling (Thomas Marsh), Fred Kohler (Deroux), Cyril Chadwick (Peter Jesson), Gladys Hulette (Ruby), James Marcus (Judge Haller), Francis Powers (Sergeant Slattery), J. Farrell McDonald (Corporal Casey), James Welch (Private Schultz), Colin Chase (Tony), Walter Rogers (General Dodge), Jack O'Brien (Dinny), George Waggner (Col. 'Buffalo Bill' Cody), John Padjan (Wild Bill Hickok), Charles O'Malley (Major North), Charles Newton (Collis P. Huntington), Delbert Mann (Charles Crocker), Chief Big Tree (Cheyenne Chief), Chief White Spear (Sioux Chief), Edward Piel (old Chinaman), James Gordon (David

Brandon, Sr.), Winston Miller (Davy, as child), Peggy Cartwright (Miriam, as child), Thomas Durant (Jack Ganzhorn), Stanhope Wheatcroft (John Hay), Frances Teague (Polka Dot), Dan Borzage.

Ford's first great success, about the race between the Union Pacific and the Central Pacific to lay tracks for the first transcontinental railroad, and centering on Davy Brandon, who, while searching for his father's murderer, romances a childhood sweetheart (her father is one of the leaders of the railway enterprise) and becomes a rail builder himself. (Working titles: *The Trans-Continental Railroad, The Iron Trail.*)

1924 HEARTS OF OAK (Fox).

Director: John Ford. Scenarist: Charles Kenyon, from play by James A. Herne. Photographer: George Schneiderman. 5,336 feet. Released: October 5. With Hobart Bosworth (Terry Dunnivan, a sea captain), Pauline Starke (Chrystal), Theodore von Eltz (Ned Fairweather), James Gordon (John Owen), Francis Powers (Grandpa Dunnivan), Jennie Lee (Grandma Dunnivan), Francis Ford.

An old sea captain sacrifices his happiness (and finally his life) for the sake of his two adopted children. Moving Picture World: '. . . *packed with realistic scenes of storms at sea, wonderful views of the Arctic land, fine shots of the New England coast country.* . . .'

1925 LIGHTNIN' (Fox).

Director: John Ford. Scenarist: Frances Marion, from play by Winchell Smith and Frank Bacon. Photographer: Joseph H. August. Assistant director: Edward O'Fearna. 8,050 feet. Released: August 23. With Jay Hunt ('Lightnin' Bill Jones), Madge Bellamy (Millie), Edythe Chapman (Mother Jones), Wallace McDonald (John Marvin), J. Farrell McDonald (Judge Townsend), Ethel Clayton (Margaret Davis), Richard Travers (Raymond Thomas), James Marcus (sheriff), Otis Harlan (Zeb), Brandon Hurst (Hammond), Peter Mazutis (Oscar).

Mother Jones runs a small hotel that straddles the California-Nevada stateline; her husband, 'Lightnin' Bill (*not* appropriately nicknamed) likes to drink and tell stories about all the things he used to be. A pair of swindlers try to get their land cheap (by first breaking up the marriage) because they know the railroad is planning to come through and will want it; but they're foiled through the efforts of the Jones's daughter and her boyfriend. *Ford's first film with Joseph August as photographer.* (*Remade in* 1930 *by Henry King.*)

1925 KENTUCKY PRIDE (Fox).

Director: John Ford. Writer: Dorothy Yost. Photographer: George Schneiderman. Assistant director: Edward O'Fearna. 6,597 feet. Released: September 6. With Henry B. Walthall (Mr Beaumont), J. Farrell McDonald (Mike Donovan),

Gertrude Astor (Mrs Beaumont), Malcolm Waite (Greve Carter), Belle Stoddard (Mrs Donovan), Winston Miller (Danny Donovan), Peaches Jackson (Virginia Beaumont), and the horses, Man O' War, Fair Play, Negofol, The Finn, Morvich, Confederacy and Virginia's Future.

A horse tells the story: Ruined (because of gambling debts) when his horse breaks her leg, Beaumont eventually enters her colt, Confederacy, in the big race and she wins; her mother has become a drayhorse, but Beaumont buys her back.

1925 THE FIGHTING HEART (Fox).

Director: John Ford. Scenarist: Lillie Hayward, from *Once to Every Man* by Larry Evans. Photographer: Joseph H. August. 6,978 feet. Released (with tinted sequences): October 18. With George O'Brien (Denny Bolton), Billie Dove (Doris Anderson), J. Farrell McDonald (Jerry), Diana Miller (Helen Van Allen), Victor McLaglen (Soapy Williams), Bert Woodruff (Grandfather Bolton), James Marcus (Judge Maynard), Lynn Cowan (Chub Morehouse), Harvey Clark (Dennison), Hank Mann (his assistant), Francis Ford (the town fool), Francis Powers (John Anderson), Hazel Howell (Oklahoma Kate), Edward Piel (Flash Fogarty).

Photoplay said, 'A prizefighter is swept to Broadway by ambition; love brings him back to Main Street. Three of the most thrilling fights ever screened.' *'Oh, that was a prize-fighting picture,' said Ford. 'In those days, we made one a month.' Victor McLaglen's first appearance in a Ford film.*

1925 THANK YOU (Fox).

Director: John Ford. Producer: John Golden. Scenarist: Frances Marion, from play by Winchell Smith and Tom Cushing. Photographer: George Schneiderman. 75 minutes. Released (with tinted sequences): November 1. With George O'Brien (Kenneth Jamieson), Jacqueline Logan (Diana Lee, the mother), Alec Francis (David Lee), J. Farrell McDonald (Andy), Cyril Chadwick (Mr Jones), Edith Bostwick (Mrs Jones), Vivian Ogden (Miss Blodgett), James Neill (Dr Cobb), Billy Rinaldi (Sweet, Jr.), Maurice Murphy (Willie Jones), Robert Milasch (Sweet, Sr.), George Fawcett (Jamieson, Sr.), Marion Harlan (Millie Jones), Ida Moore, Frankie Bailey (gossips).

Two vestrymen, trying to stop a clergyman from getting a pay raise, provoke a scandal that implicates his niece. But the banker's son, whom the clergyman reformed, proves her innocence.

1926 THE SHAMROCK HANDICAP (Fox).

Director: John Ford. Scenarist: John Stone, from story by Peter B. Kyne. Photographer: George

Schneiderman. Assistant director: Edward O'Fearna. 5,685 feet. Released (with tinted sequences): May 2. With Janet Gaynor (Sheila Gaffney), Leslie Fenton (Neil Ross), J. Farrell McDonald (Dennis O'Shea), Louis Payne (Sir Miles Gaffney), Claire McDowell (Molly O'Shea), Willard Louis (Martin Finch), Andy Clark (Chesty Morgan), Georgie Harris (Benny Ginsberg), Ely Reynolds (Puss), Thomas Delmar (Michael), Brandon Hurst (the procurer).

An old Irish nobleman is so considerate of his tenants regarding rent that his financial position finally forces him to sell part of his stable to an American, who takes the Irishman's young jockey back with him to the States. When the boy is crippled in a race, his former employer, together with his daughter and their prize filly, come to America. They enter the horse in the $25,000 Shamrock Handicap, which she wins, and they all go home to Ireland.

1926 3 BAD MEN (Fox).

Director: John Ford. Scenarists: Ford, John Stone, from the novel, *Over the Border*, by Herman Whitaker. Photographer: George Schneiderman. Filmed at Jackson Hole, Wyoming, and in the Mojave Desert. 8,710 feet. Released (with tinted sequences): August 28. With George O'Brien (Dan O'Malley), Olive Borden (Lee Carlton), J. Farrell McDonald (Mike Costigan), Tom Santschi (Bull Stanley), Frank Campeau (Spade Allen), Lou Tellegen (Sheriff Layne Hunter), George Harris (Joe Minsk), Jay Hunt (old prospector), Priscilla Bonner (Millie Stanley), Otis Harlan (Zack Leslie), Walter Perry (Pat Monahan), Grace Gordon (Millie's friend), Alec B. Francis (Rev. Calvin Benson), George Irving (General Neville), Phyllis Haver (Prairie Beauty), Vester Pegg, Bud Osborne.

One of Ford's most important silents: In the Dakota Territory of 1876, as thousands arrive for the Dakota land rush, three 'bad' men first serve as match-makers for a young couple and later give up their lives to save them from a corrupt sheriff and his gang.

1926 THE BLUE EAGLE (Fox).

Director: John Ford. Scenarist: L. G. Rigby, from story, 'The Lord's Referee,' by Gerald Beaumont. Photographer: George Schneiderman. Assistant director: Edward O'Fearna. 6,200 feet. Released (with tinted sequences): September 12. With George O'Brien (George D'Arcy), Janet Gaynor (Rose Cooper), William Russell (Big Tim Ryan), Robert Edeson (Father Joe), David Butler (Nick Galvani), Phillip Ford (Limpy D'Arcy), Ralph Sipperly (Slats Mulligan), Margaret Livingston (Mary Rohan), Jerry Madden (Baby Tom), Harry Tenbrook (Bascom), Lew Short (Captain McCarthy).

Rivals as civilians, and both in love with the same girl,

gang leaders D'Arcy and Ryan continue their feud in the Navy, where only military discipline keeps them in check. The battleship chaplain (who was also their parish priest) finally decides to let them fight it out in the ring, but the match is interrupted by a submarine attack. After the war, when the same gang of dope smugglers kills D'Arcy's brother and shoots one of Ryan's pals, the two call a truce to rout the criminals, and then go right back to fighting each other.

1927 UPSTREAM (Fox).

Director: John Ford. Scenarist: Randall H. Faye, from story 'The Snake's Wife,' by Wallace Smith. Photographer: Charles G. Clarke. Assistant director: Edward O'Fearna. 5,510 feet. Released: January 30. With Nancy Nash (Gertie King), Earle Foxe (Brasingham), Grant Withers (Jack LeVelle), Raymond Hitchcock (The Star Border), Lydia Yeamans Titus (Miss Breckenbridge), Emile Chautard (Campbell Mandare), Ted McNamara, Sammy Cohen (a dance team), Francis Ford (juggler), Judy King, Lillian Worth (sister team), Jane Winton (soubrette), Harry Bailey (Gus Hoffman), Ely Reynolds (Deerfoot).

A comedy-drama about a group of actors in a London boarding house: Brasingham is chosen to play 'Hamlet' in a West End revival, and its success goes to his head; he condescends to flirt with his former sweetheart and her husband throws him out on his ear.

1928 MOTHER MACHREE (Fox).

Director: John Ford. Scenarist: Gertrude Orr, from story by Rida Johnson Young. Photographer: Chester Lyons. Editors and title-writers: Katherine Hilliker, H. H. Caldwell. Assistant director: Edward O'Fearna. 75 minutes. Released (with tinted sequences): January 22; (with music and synchronized sound effects): October 21. With Belle Bennett (Ellen McHugh), Neil Hamilton (Brian McHugh), Philippe De Lacy (Brian, as child), Pat Somerset (Robert De Puyster), Victor McLaglen (Terrence O'Dowd), Ted McNamara (Harpist of Wexford), John MacSweeney (Irish priest), Eulalie Jensen (Rachel van Studdiford), Constance Howard (Edith Cutting), Ethel Clayton (Mrs Cutting), William Platt (Pips), Jacques Rollens (Signor Bellini), Rodney Hildebrand (Brian McHugh, Sr.), Joyce Wirard (Edith Cutting, as child), Robert Parrish (child).

A Madame X story: an Irish mother in America (at the turn of the century) gives up her son in the interests of his future, becomes a housekeeper and raises her employers' daughter. Years later, when this girl and her son fall in love, the boy and his mother are finally reunited.

1928 FOUR SONS (Fox).

Director: John Ford. Scenarist: Philip Klein, from

126

story, Grandma Bernle Learns Her Letters, by I. A. R. Wylie. Photographers: George Schneiderman, Charles G. Clarke. Music arranger: S. L. Rothafel. Theme, 'Little Mother,' by Erno Rapee, Lew Pollack. Editor: Margaret V. Clancey. Title-writers: Katherine Hilliker, H. H. Caldwell. Assistant director: Edward O'Fearna. 100 minutes. Released (with music and synchronized sound effects): February 13. With Margaret Mann (Frau Bernle), James Hall (Joseph Bernle), Charles Morton (Johann Bernle), George Meeker (Andres Bernle), Francis X. Bushman, Jr. (Franz Bernle), June Collyer (Annabelle Bernle), Albert Gran (postman), Earle Foxe (Major Von Stomm), Frank Reicher (headmaster), Jack Pennick (Joseph's American friend), Archduke Leopold of Austria (German captain), Hughie Mack (innkeeper), Wendell Franklin (James Henry), Auguste Tollaire (Mayor), Ruth Mix (Johann's girl), Robert Parrish (child), Michael Mark (Von Stomm's orderly), L. J. O'Conner (Aubergiste), Ferdinand Schumann-Heink, Capt. John Porters, Carl Boheme, Constant Franke, Hans Furberg, Tibor von Janny, Stanley Blystone, Lieut. George Blagoi (officers).

The story of a Bavarian mother's four sons—the one who goes to America, and the three who remain in Europe and are killed in the First World War. At the end, the mother joins her only remaining son and his family in the United States. Ford's biggest success since The Iron Horse.

1928 HANGMAN'S HOUSE (Fox).

Director: John Ford. Scenarists: Marion Orth, Willard Mack, from novel by Brian Oswald Donn-Byrne, adapted by Philip Klein. Photographer: George Schneidermann. Editor: Margaret V. Clancey. Title-writer: Malcolm Stuart Boylan. Assistant director: Phil Ford. 7 reels. Released: May 13. With Victor McLaglen (Citizen Hogan), Hobart Bosworth (James O'Brien, Lord Chief Justice), June Collyer (Connaught O'Brien), Larry Kent (Dermott McDermott), Earle Foxe (John Darcy), Eric Mayne (Legionnaire Colonel), Joseph Burke (Neddy Joe), Belle Stoddard (Anne McDermott), John Wayne (spectator at horse race).

Ireland. 'Hanging Judge' O'Brien is dying; because he thinks it will give her position, he forces his daughter, Connaught, to marry Darcy. But she loves Dermott. An exiled Irish patriot named Hogan solves their dilemma: risking his life, he returns to Ireland to kill a man who married then deserted his sister and caused her suicide—that man is Darcy. There is a horse race in the story that anticipates—in fact betters—the one in The Quiet Man, with John Wayne (in his first of almost twenty Ford films) as an over-enthusiastic spectator who smashes a picket fence in his excitement. 'The only shot I remember,' said Ford, 'is of the Gaelic cross, with the people passing in front of it.'

1928 NAPOLEON'S BARBER (Fox-Movietone).

Director: John Ford. Scenarist: Arthur Caesar,

from his own play. Photographer: George Schneiderman. Title-writer: Malcolm Stuart Boylan. 32 minutes. Released: November 24. With Otto Matiesen (Napoleon), Frank Reicher (The Barber), Natalie Golitzin (Josephine), Helen Ware (Barber's wife), Philippe De Lacy (Barber's son), Russell Powell (blacksmith), D'Arcy Corrigan (tailor), Michael Mark (peasant), Buddy Roosevelt, Ervin Renard, Joe Waddell, Youcca-Troubetzkoy (French officers), Henry Herbert (soldier).

Ford's first talkie, about a barber who brags to a customer what he'd do to Napoleon if he had the chance and discovers the customer *is* Napoleon.

1928 RILEY THE COP (Fox).

Director: John Ford. Writers: James Gruen, Fred Stanley. Photographer: Charles G. Clarke. Editor: Alex Troffey. Assistant director: Phil Ford. 67 minutes. Released (with music and synchronized sound effects): November 25. With J. Farrell McDonald (Aloysius Riley), Louise Fazenda (Lena Krausmeyer), Nancy Drexel (Mary Coronelli), David Rollins (Joe Smith), Harry Schultz (Hans Krausmeyer), Billy Bevan (Paris cabdriver), Tom Wilson (Sergeant), Otto H. Fries (Munich cab driver), Mildred Boyd (Caroline), Ferdinand Schumann-Heink (Julius), Del Henderson (Judge Coronelli), Russell Powell (Kuchendorf), Mike Donlin (crook), Robert Parrish.

New York. Prohibition. Riley, unlike his rival Krausmeyer, is a cop who has never arrested anyone, and he's very fond of Davy and Mary, a young pair of lovers he's known since they were born. When Mary goes to Germany, Davy follows, and Riley is sent to Munich to bring him back—on an embezzling charge. But there's beer over there! And a fraulein named Lena. It's everything Davy can do to get *Riley* on the ship back—and Lena goes with them. Davy is exonerated, and Lena—turns out to be Krausmeyer's sister. *'That was a story that had actually happened,'* said Ford, *'and I thought it was a funny idea.'*

1929 STRONG BOY (Fox).

Director: John Ford. Scenarists: James Kevin McGuiness, Andrew Bennison, John McLain, from story by Frederick Hazlett Brennan. Photographer: Joseph H. August. Title-writer: Malcolm Stuart Boylan. 63 minutes. Released (with music and synchronized sound effects): March 3. With Victor McLaglen (William 'Strong Boy' Bloss), Leatrice Joy (Mary McGregor), Clyde Cook (Pete), Slim Summerville (Slim), Kent Sanderson (Wilbur Watkins), Tom Wilson (baggage master), Jack Pennick (baggageman), Eulalie Jensen (The Queen), David Torrence (railroad

president), J. Farrell McDonald (Angus McGregor), Dolores Johnson (usherette), Douglas Scott (Wobby), Robert Ryan (porter).

'Strong Boy' would like to please his girl and make something more of himself than a baggage porter, but all his efforts fail and he winds up a locomotive engineer just like her father. When a gang of train robbers tries to steal the jewels of visiting royalty, however, 'Strong Boy' outwits them and finally becomes a hero.

1929 THE BLACK WATCH (Fox).

Directors: John Ford, ('staged by') Lumsden Hare. Scenarists: James Kevin McGuiness, John Stone, from novel, *King of the Khyber Rifles*, by Talbot Mundy. Photographer: Joseph H. August. Song, "Flowers of Delight" by William Kernell. Editor: Alex Troffey. Assistant director: Edward O'Fearna. 93 minutes. Released: May 8. With Victor McLaglen (Capt. Donald King), Myrna Loy (Yasmani), Roy D'Arcy (Rewa Ghunga), Pat Somerset (Highlanders' officer), David Rollins (Lt. Malcolm King), Mitchell Lewis (Mohammed Khan), Walter Long (Harem Bey), David Percy (Highlanders' officer), Lumsden Hare (Colonel), Cyril Chadwick (Major Twynes), David Torrence (Marechal), Francis Ford (Major MacGregor), Claude King (General in India), Frederick Sullivan (general's aide), Joseph Diskay (Muezzin), Richard Travers (adjutant), Joyzelle.

A British army officer, Capt. King of The Black Watch, is thought to be a coward when he goes to India immediately after the outbreak of World War I. Actually he is on a secret mission to locate and free some captured fellow soldiers. *Ford's first feature-length talkie is almost destroyed by the interminable dialogue scenes that Hare directed. (Remade by Henry King as* King of the Khyber Rifles, 1954.)

1929 SALUTE (Fox).

Director: John Ford. Scenarist: James K. McGuinness, from story by Tristram Tupper, John Stone. Photographer: Joseph H. August. Editor: Alex Troffey. Title-writer: Wilbur Morse, Jr. Assistant directors: Edward O'Fearna, R. L. Hough. Filmed at Annapolis, Maryland. 86 minutes. Released: September 1. With George O'Brien (Cadet John Randall), Helen Chandler (Nancy Wayne), Stepin' Fetchit (Smoke Screen), William Janney (Midshipman Paul Randall), Frank Albertson (Midshipman Albert Edward Price), Joyce Compton (Marion Wilson), Cliff Dempsey (Maj. Gen. Somers), Lumsden Hare (Rear Admiral Randall), David Butler (Navy Coach), Rex Bell (Cadet), John Breeden (Midshipman), Ward Bond, John Wayne (football players).

Army-Navy rivalry as personified by a West Point cadet with a kid brother at Annapolis: John (Army) makes a pass at (Navy) Paul's girl just to get Paul to appreciate her. But Paul doesn't know that, and tries to get even with John in the climactic football game, which ends, appropriately, in a tie. *Ward Bond's first appearance in a Ford film.*

1930 MEN WITHOUT WOMEN (Fox).

Director: John Ford, ('staged by') Andrew Bennison. Scenarist: Dudley Nichols, from story, 'Submarine,' by Ford, James K. McGuinness. Photographer: Joseph H. August. Art director: William S. Darling. Music: Peter Brunelli, Glen Knight. Editor: Paul Weatherwax. Assistant director: Edward O'Fearna. Technical advisor: Schuyler E. Grey. 77 minutes. Released: January 31. With Kenneth MacKenna ('Burke'), Frank Albertson ('Price'), Paul Page ('Handsome'), Pat Somerset (Lt. Digby, R.N.), Walter McGrail (Cobb), Stuart Erwin (Jenkins, radio operator), Warren Hymer (Kaufman), J. Farrell McDonald (Costello), Roy Stewart (Capt. Carson), Warner Richmond (Lt. Commander Bridewell), Harry Tenbrook (Winkler), Ben Hendricks, Jr. (Murphy), George Le Guere (Pollosk), Charles Gerard (Commander Weymouth, R.N.), John Wayne, Robert Parrish.

Fourteen men are trapped in a submarine; finally, one man must stay behind so the others can escape. *Ford's first film with Dudley Nichols.*

1930 BORN RECKLESS (Fox).

Directors: John Ford, ('staged by') Andrew Bennison. Scenarist: Dudley Nichols, from novel, *Louis Beretti*, by Donald Henderson Clarke. Photographer: George Schneiderman. Art director: Jack Schulze. Associate producer: James K. McGuinness. Editor: Frank E. Hull. Assistant director: Edward O'Fearna. 82 minutes. Released: May 11. With Edmund Lowe (Louis Beretti), Catherine Dale Owen (Joan Sheldon), Lee Tracy (Bill O'Brien), Marguerite Churchill (Rosa Beretti), Warren Hymer (Big Shot), Pat Somerset (Duke), William Harrigan (Good News Brophy), Frank Albertson (Frank Sheldon), Ferike Boros (Ma Beretti), J. Farrell McDonald (District Attorney), Paul Porcasi (Pa Beretti), Eddie Gribbon (Bugs), Mike Donlin (Fingy Moscovitz), Ben Bard (Joe Bergman), Paul Page (Ritzy Reilly), Joe Brown (Needle Beer Grogan), Jack Pennick, Ward Bond (soldiers), Roy Stewart (District Attorney Cardigan), Yola D'Avril (French girl).

A comedy-drama about a New York gangster who is sent to fight in the war as a vote-getting gesture by a political-minded judge. The gangster returns and picks up where he left off. *'Andy [Bennison] was a friend of ours,' said Ford, 'so we said he could rehearse the actors. After he'd been working four days, I went in and he was still on the first scene—and he was stark staring drunk. So I sent him home. Next day he was all right.'* One suspects Ford is actually being kind; the dialogue scenes are so stiff that it's difficult to believe Ford could have directed them and at the same time made a sequence like the freewheeling war interlude.

1930 UP THE RIVER (Fox).

Director: John Ford, ('staged by') William Collier, Jr. Writer:

Maurine Watkins (and uncredited: Ford, William Collier, Sr.). Photographer: Joseph H. August. Set designer: Duncan Cramer. Music and lyrics: Joseph McCarthy, James F. Hanley. Wardrobe: Sophie Wachner. Editor: Frank E. Hull. Assistant directors: Edward O'Fearna, Wingate Smith. 92 minutes. Released: October 12. With Spencer Tracy (St. Louis), Warren Hymer (Dannemora Dan), Humphrey Bogart (Steve), Claire Luce (Judy), Joan Lawes (Jean), Sharon Lynn (Edith La Verne), George McFarlane (Jessup), Gaylord Pendleton (Morris), Morgan Wallace (Frosby), William Collier, Sr. (Pop), Robert E. O'Connor (guard), Louise. MacIntosh (Mrs Massey), Edythe Chapman (Mrs Jordan), Johnny Walker (Happy), Noel Francis (Sophie), Mildred Vincent (Annie), Wilbur Mack (Whitelay), Goodee Montgomery (Kit), Althea Henley (Cynthia), Carol Wines (Daisy Elmore), Adele Windsor (Minnie), Richard Keene (Dick), Elizabeth and Helen Keating (May and June), Robert Burns (Slim), John Swor (Clem), Pat Somerset (Beauchamp), Joe Brown (Deputy Warden), Harvey Clark (Nash), Black and Blue (Slim and Klem), Morgan Wallace (Fosby), Robert Parrish.

A comedy about two convicts who don't really mind prison—especially since they can break out any time they like. (*Remade in 1938 by Alfred Werker.*)

1931 SEAS BENEATH (Fox).

Director: John Ford. Scenarist: Dudley Nichols, from story by James Parker, Jr. Photographer: Joseph H. August. Editor: Frank E. Hull. 99 minutes. Released: January 30. With George O'Brien (Commander Bob Kingsley, USN), Marion Lessing (Anna M. Von Steuben), Warren Hymer ('Lug' Kaufman), William Collier, Sr. ('Mugs' O'Flaherty), John Loder (Franz Schilling), Walter C. 'Judge' Kelly (Chief Mike Costello), Walter McGrail (Joe Cobb), Henry Victor (Ernst Von Steuben, Commandant, U-boat 172), Mona Maris (Lolita), Larry Kent (Lt. MacGregor), Gaylord Pendleton (Ensign Dick Cabot), Nat Pendleton ('Butch' Wagner), Harry Tenbrook (Winkler), Terry Ray (Reilly), Hans Furberg (Fritz Kampf, second officer, U-172), Ferdinand Schumann-Heink (Adolph Brucker, Engineer, U-172), Francis Ford (Trawler Captain), Kurt Furberg (Hoffman), Ben Hall (Harrigan), Harry Weil (Jevinsky), Maurice Murphy (Merkel).

A story about the operation of one of the Q boats—the 'mystery ships' used by America to search out and destroy enemy submarines during the First World War.

1931 THE BRAT (Fox).

Director: John Ford. Scenarists: Sonya Levien, S. N. Behrman, Maude Fulton, from play by Fulton. Photographer: Joseph H. August. Editor: Alex Troffey. 81 minutes. Released: August 23. With Sally O'Neil (The Brat), Alan Dinehart (MacMillan Forester), Frank Albertson (Stephen Forester), Virginia

Cherrill (Angela), June Collyer (Jane), J. Farrell McDonald (Timson, the Butler), William Collier Sr. (Judge), Margaret Mann (housekeeper), Albert Gran (Bishop), Mary Forbes (Mrs Forester), Louise MacIntosh (Lena).

An affected society novelist picks up a waif in night court and takes her home as 'research' for his next book; his family is scandalized, especially when romantic complications set in.

1931 ARROWSMITH (Goldwyn-United Artists).

Director: John Ford. Producer: Samuel Goldwyn. Scenarist: Sidney Howard, from novel by Sinclair Lewis. Photographer: Ray June. Art director: Richard Day. Music: Alfred Newman. Editor: Hugh Bennett. 108 minutes. Released: December 1. With Ronald Colman (Dr Martin Arrowsmith), Helen Hayes (Leora), A. E. Anson (Prof. Gottlieb), Richard Bennett (Sondelius), Claude King (Dr Tubbs), Beulah Bondi (Mrs Tozer), Myrna Loy (Joyce Lanyon), Russell Hopton (Terry Wickett), De Witt Jennings (Mr Tozer), John Qualen (Henry Novak), Adele Watson (Mrs Novak), Lumsden Hare (Sir Robert Fairland), Bert Roach (Bert Tozer), Charlotte Henry (a young girl), Clarence Brooks (Oliver Marchand), Walter Downing (City Clerk), David Landau, James Marcus, Alec B. Francis, Sidney McGrey, Florence Britton, Bobby Watson.

An idealistic young doctor fights against the hypocrisies of his colleagues, and finally goes to the tropics in order to continue his research for a serum. During a terrible epidemic, his wife dies. *Ford's first film away from Fox since 1921: 'Sam Goldwyn borrowed me to do it,' says Ford. 'It was a good story and I think it's still a very modern picture.'*

1932 AIR MAIL (Universal).

Director: John Ford. Producer: Carl Laemmle, Jr. Scenarists: Dale Van Every, Lt. Commander Frank W. Wead, from story by Wead. Photographer: Karl Freund. Special effects: John P. Fulton. Aerial stunts: Paul Mantz. 83 minutes. Released: November 3. With Pat O'Brien (Duke Talbot), Ralph Bellamy (Mike Miller), Gloria Stuart (Ruth Barnes), Lillian Bond (Irene Wilkins), Russell Hopton ('Dizzy' Wilkins), Slim Summerville ('Slim' McCune), Frank Albertson (Tommy Bogan), Leslie Fenton (Tony Dressel), David Landau ('Pop'), Tom Corrigan ('Sleepy' Collins), William Daly ('Tex' Lane), Hans Furberg ('Heinie' Kramer), Lew Kelly (drunkard), Frank Beal, Francis Ford, James Donlan, Louise MacIntosh, Katherine Perry (passengers), Beth Milton (plane attendant), Edmund Burns (radio announcer), Charles

de la Montte, Lt. Pat Davis (passenger plane pilots), Jim Thorpe (Indian), Enrico Caruso, Jr., Billy Thorpe, Alene Carroll, Jack Pennick.

A story of the early days of air mail flying, and the conflicts between an incorrigibly reckless pilot and his more sober superior. *'Slim Summerville wasn't even in the script,' Ford said, 'so we put him in sweeping the floor, got a few laughs out of him. There was some great flying by Paul Mantz—it was his first job.'* It was also Ford's first picture with Frank ('Spig') Wead, whom he was to immortalize twenty-five years later in The Wings of Eagles.

1932 FLESH (Metro-Goldwyn-Mayer).

Director: John Ford. Scenarists: Leonard Praskins, Edgar Allen Woolf and (uncredited) William Faulkner, from story by Edmund Goulding. Dialogue: Moss Hart. Photographer: Arthur Edeson. Editor: William S. Gray. 95 minutes. Released: December 9. With Wallace Beery (Polakai), Karen Morley (Lora), Ricardo Cortez (Nicky), Jean Hersholt (Mr Herman), John Miljan (Joe Willard), Vince Barnett (waiter), Herman Bing (Pepi), Greta Meyer (Mrs Herman), Ed Brophy (Dolan), Ward Bond, Nat Pendleton.

A German wrestler comes to America where he is exploited by unscrupulous racketeers as well as by the girl he loves.

1933 PILGRIMAGE (Fox).

Director: John Ford. Scenarists: Philip Klein, Barry Connors, from story 'Gold Star Mother,' by I. A. R. Wylie. Dialogue: Dudley Nichols. Photographer: George Schneiderman. Art director: William Darling. Music: R. H. Bassett. Editor: Louis R. Loeffler. Assistant director: Edward O'Fearna. Dialogue director: William Collier, Sr. 90 minutes. Released: July 12. With Henrietta Grosman (Hannah Jessop), Heather Angel (Suzanne), Norman Foster (Jim Jessop), Marian Nixon (Mary Saunders), Maurice Murphy (Gary Worth), Lucille Laverne (Mrs Hatfield), Charley Grapewin (Dad Saunders), Hedda Hopper (Mrs Worth), Robert Warwick (Maj. Albertson), Betty Blythe (Janet Prescot), Francis Ford (Mayor), Louise Carter (Mrs Rogers), Jay Ward (Jim Saunders), Francis Rich (nurse), Adele Watson (Mrs. Simms).

A possessive mother forbids her son's marriage to the girl he loves and has made pregnant, driving the boy into the Army and the First World War, during which he is killed. Years later, still unrelenting toward the girl and her illegitimate grandchild, she makes a pilgrimage along with a group of other Gold Star Mothers to her son's grave in France. An encounter there with a young man whose experiences with *his* mother mirror the woman's own story, makes her realize her tragic mistakes.

1933 DR BULL (Fox).
Director: John Ford. Scenarist: Paul Green, from novel, *The Last Adam*, by James Gould Cozzens. Dialogue: Jane Storm. Photographer: George Schneiderman. Music: Samuel Kaylin. 76 minutes. Released: September 22. With Will Rogers (Dr Bull), Marian Nixon (May Tripping), Berton Churchill (Herbert Banning), Louise Dresser (Mrs Banning), Howard Lally (Joe Tripping), Rochelle Hudson (Virginia Banning), Vera Allen (Janet Carmaker), Tempe Pigotte (Grandma), Elizabeth Patterson (Aunt Patricia), Ralph Morgan (Dr Verney), Andy Devine (Larry Ward), Nora Cecil (Aunt Emily), Patsy O'Byrne (Susan), Effie Ellsler (Aunt Myra), Veda Buckland (Mary), Helen Freeman (Helen Upjohn), Robert Parrish.

Ford's first of three major films with Will Rogers, about a doctor in a small Connecticut town, his patients' petty illnesses, and the terrible epidemic that strikes the community. (Working title: *Life's Worth Living*.)

1934 THE LOST PATROL (RKO Radio).
Director: John Ford. Executive producer: Merian C. Cooper. Associate producer: Cliff Reid. Scenarists: Dudley Nichols, Garrett Fort, from story, 'Patrol,' by Philip MacDonald. Photographer: Harold Wenstrom. Art directors: Van Nest Polglase, Sidney Ullman. Music: Max Steiner. Editor: Paul Weatherwax. Filmed in the Yuma desert. 74 minutes. Released: February 16. With Victor McLaglen (The Sergeant), Boris Karloff (Sanders), Wallace Ford (Morelli), Reginald Denny (George Brown), J. M. Kerrigan (Quincannon), Billy Bevan (Herbert Hale), Alan Hale (Cook), Brandon Hurst (Bell), Douglas Walton (Pearson), Sammy Stein (Abelson), Howard Wilson (flyer), Neville Clark (Lt. Hawkins), Paul Hanson (Jock Mackay), Francis Ford.

During World War I a British platoon gets lost in the Mesopotamian Desert. Unseen Arabs pick them off one by one, until only the Sergeant is alive when help comes. (*Max Steiner won the Oscar for Best Score.*)

1934 THE WORLD MOVES ON (Fox).
Director: John Ford. Producer: Winfield Sheehan. Writer: Reginald C. Berkeley. Photographer: George Schneiderman. Art director: William Darling. Set decorator: Thomas Little. Costumes: Rita Kaufman Music: Max Steiner, Louis De Francesco, R. H. Bassett, David Buttolph, Hugo Friedhofer, George Gershwin. Songs: 'Should She Desire Me Not', by

De Francesco, 'Ave Maria,' by Charles Gounod. 90 minutes. Released: June 27. With Madeleine Carroll (Mrs Warburton, 1824; Mary Warburton, 1914), Franchot Tone (Richard Girard, 1924 and 1914), Lumsden Hare (Gabriel Warburton, 1824; Sir John Warburton, 1914), Raul Roulien (Carlos Girard, 1824; Henri Girard, 1914), Reginald Denny (Erik Von Gerhardt), Siegfried Rumann (Baron Von Gerhardt), Louise Dresser (Baroness Von Gerhardt), Stepin' Fetchit (Dixie), Dudley Diggs (Mr Manning), Frank Melton (John Girard, 1824), Brenda Fowler (Mrs Girard, 1824), Russell Simpson (notary public, 1824), Walter McGrail (French duelist, 1824), Marcelle Corday (Miss Girard, 1824), Charles Bastin (Jacques Girard, 1914), Barry Norton (Jacques Girard, 1929), George Irving (Charles Girard, 1914), Ferdinand Schumann-Heink (Fritz Von Gerhardt), Georgette Rhodes (Jeanne Girard, 1914), Claude King (Braithwaite), Ivan Simpson (Clumber), Frank Moran (Culbert), Jack Pennick, Francis Ford (legionnaires), Torbin Mayer (German Chamberlain, 1914).

The 100-year history (1824–1924) of a powerful Louisiana dynasty—beginning with the patriarch's will —which sends sons off to manage French, German and English branches of the business—and ending after the descendants have recovered from their collapse caused by World War I.

1934 JUDGE PRIEST (Fox).
Director: John Ford. Producer: Sol Wurtzel. Scenarists: Dudley Nichols, Lamar Trotti, from stories by Irvin S. Cobb. Photographer: George Schneiderman. Music: Samuel Kaylin. 80 minutes. Released: October 5. With Will Rogers (Judge William 'Billy' Priest), Henry B. Walthall (Rev. Ashby Brand), Tom Brown (Jerome Priest), Anita Louise (Ellie May Gillespie), Rochelle Hudson (Virginia Maydew), Berton Churchill (Senator Horace K. Maydew), David Landau (Bob Gillis), Brenda Fowler (Mrs Caroline Priest), Hattie McDaniel (Aunt Dilsey), Stepin' Fetchit (Jeff Poindexter), Frank Melton (Flem Tally), Roger Imhof (Billy Gaynor), Charley Grapewin (Sgt. Jimmy Bagby), Francis Ford (Juror No. 12), Paul McAllister (Doc Lake), Matt McHugh (Gabby Rives), Hy Meyer (Herman Feldsburg), Louis Mason (Sheriff Birdsong), Robert Parrish.

1890. A small Kentucky town that hasn't forgotten the Civil War. When Gillis is brought to trial for a murderous assault, it is the Rev. Brand's testimony, recounting Gillis' heroism in the Virginia Regiment, that finally wins the man's acquittal from a jury of Confederate veterans. *Ford was to use the same characters and many elements from this film in* The Sun Shines Bright (1953).

1935 THE WHOLE TOWN'S TALKING (Columbia).

Director: John Ford. Producer: Lester Cowan. Scenarist: Jo Swerling, from novel by W. R. Burnett. Dialogue: Robert Riskin. Photographer: Joseph H. August. Editor: Viola Lawrence. Assistant director: Wilbur McGaugh. 95 minutes. Released: February 22. With Edward G. Robinson (Arthur Ferguson Jones; 'Killer' Mannion), Jean Arthur (Miss 'Bill' Clark), Wallace Ford (Mr Healy), Arthur Byron (Mr Spencer), Arthur Hohl (Det. Sgt Michael Boyle), Donald Meek (Mr Hoyt), Paul Harvey (J. G. Carpenter), Edward Brophy ('Slugs' Martin), J. Farrell McDonald (Warden), Etienne Girardot (Mr Seaver), James Donlan (Howe), John Wray (Henchman), Effie Ellsler (Aunt Agatha), Robert Emmett O'Connor (Police Lt.), Joseph Sawyer, Francis Ford, Robert Parrish.

A timid little clerk is a dead ringer for a notorious gangster. When the latter escapes from jail, the clerk is picked up instead, and thus becomes a celebrity in his own right. The gangster decides to rub him out and take over his identity, but, needless to say, he fails. *Ford: 'It was all right—I never saw it.'* (Working title: *Passport to Fame*).

1935 THE INFORMER (RKO Radio).

Director: John Ford. Associate producer: Cliff Reid. Scenarist: Dudley Nichols, from novel by Liam O'Flaherty. Photographer: Joseph H. August. Art directors: Van Nest Polglase, Charles Kirk. Set decorator: Julia Heron. Costumes: Walter Plunkett. Music: Max Steiner. Editor: George Hively. 91 minutes. Released: May 1. With Victor McLaglen (Gypo Nolan), Heather Angel (Mary McPhillip), Preston Foster (Dan Gallagher), Margot Grahame (Kattie Madden), Wallace Ford (Frankie McPhillip), Una O'Connor (Mrs McPhillip), J. M. Kerrigan (Terry), Joseph Sawyer (Bartley Muiholland), Neil Fitzgerald (Tommy Conner), Donald Meek (Pat Mulligan), D'Arcy Corrigan (The Blindman), Leo McCabe (Donahue), Gaylord Pendleton (Daley), Francis Ford ('Judge' Flynn), May Boley (Mrs Betty), Grizelda Harvey (an obedient girl), Dennis O'Dea (street singer), Jack Mulhall (look-out), Robert Parrish (soldier), Clyde Cook, Barlowe Borland, Frank Moran, Arthur McLaglen.

Dublin. 1922. During the Sinn Fein rebellion, Gypo Nolan turns a friend in to the police because he wants the reward money to go to America. *Ford's greatest critical success to that time, the film won him both the Academy Award and the New York Film Critics Award for Best Direction. (Oscars also went to McLaglen, Nichols and Steiner.)*

1935 STEAMBOAT ROUND THE BEND (20th Century-Fox).

Director: John Ford. Producer: Sol M. Wurtzel. Scenarists: Dudley Nichols, Lamar Trotti, from story by Ben Lucian Burman. Photographer: George Schneiderman. Art director: William Darling. Set decorator: Albert Hogsett. Music director: Samuel Kaylin. Editor: Alfred De Gaetano. Assistant director: Edward O'Fearna. 80 minutes. Released: September 6. With Will Rogers (Dr John Pearly), Anne Shirley (Fleety Belle), Eugene Pallette (Sheriff Rufe Jeffers), John McGuire (Duke), Berton Churchill (The New Moses), Stepin' Fetchit (George Lincoln Washington), Francis Ford (Efe), Irvin S. Cobb (Capt. Eli), Roger Imhof (Pappy), Raymond Hatton (Matt Abel), Hobart Bosworth (Chaplain), Louis Mason (boat race organizer), Charles B. Middleton (Fleety's father), Si Jenks (a drunk), Jack Pennick (Ringleader of boat attack).

Dr John sells a sure-fire cure-all medicine along the Mississippi, and somehow acquires an old steamboat, which he converts into a floating waxworks museum. When his nephew is convicted of a murder, John steams down the river looking for the only eye-witness who can prove it was self-defence. The big steamboat contest at the end is also a race to save the boy from hanging, and with the help of some unorthodox fuel (the waxworks and the doctor's highly alcoholic patent medicine), John wins both. *One of Ford's key 'thirties films and Rogers' last film. (Working title: Steamboat Bill.) During the shooting, Fox merged with Darryl Zanuck's company, 20th Century Pictures.*

1936 THE PRISONER OF SHARK ISLAND (20th Century-Fox).

Director: John Ford. Producer: Darryl F. Zanuck. Associate producer-scenarist: Nunnally Johnson, from life of Dr Samuel A. Mudd. Photography: Bert Glennon. Art director: William Darling. Set decorator: Thomas Little. Music director: Louis Silvers. Editor: Jack Murray. Assistant director: Edward O'Fearna. 95 minutes. Released: February 12. With Warner Baxter (Dr Samuel A. Mudd), Gloria Stuart (Mrs Peggy Mudd), Claude Gillingwater (Col. Dyer), Arthur Byron (Mr Ericson), O. P. Heggie (Dr. McIntyre), Harry Carey (Cdt. of Fort Jefferson, 'Shark Island'), Francis Ford (Corporal O'Toole), John Carradine (Sgt Rankin), Frank McGlynn, Sr. (Abraham Lincoln), Douglas Wood (Gen. Ewing), Joyce Kay (Martha Mudd), Fred Kohler, Jr. (Sgt Cooper), Francis McDonald (John Wilkes Booth), John McGuire (Lt. Lovell), Ernest Whitman (Buckland Montmorency 'Buck' Tilford), Paul Fix (David Herold), Frank

Shannon (Holt), Leila McIntyre (Mrs Lincoln), Etta McDaniel (Rosabelle Tilford), Arthur Loft (carpetbagger), Paul McVey (Gen. Hunter), Maurice Murphy (orderly), Jack Pennick (soldier who sends flag messages), J. M. Kerrigan (Judge Maiben), Whitney Bourne, Robert Parrish.

The true story of Samuel Mudd, the doctor who treated John Wilkes Booth—unaware that the man had just shot President Lincoln—and was tried as an accomplice in the assassination and sentenced to life imprisonment at Ft. Jefferson. His heroism during a yellow fever epidemic was instrumental in having his case re-opened, which resulted in his exoneration. (*Unofficial remake*, Hellgate, *directed in 1952 by Charles M. Warren.*)

1936 *The Last Outlaw* (RKO Radio). Director: Christy Cabanne. Scenarists: John Twist, Jack Townley, from story by John Ford and E. Murray Campbell. Editor: George Hively. 62 minutes. Released: June 19. With Harry Carey, Hoot Gibson, Tom Tyler, Henry B. Walthall.

A remake of Ford's 1919 two-reeler.

1936 MARY OF SCOTLAND (RKO Radio). Director: John Ford. Producer: Pandro S. Berman. Scenarist: Dudley Nichols, from play by Maxwell Anderson. Photography: Joseph H. August. Art directors: Van Nest Polglase, Carroll Clark. Set decorator: Darrell Silvera. Costumes: Walter Plunkett. Music: Max Steiner. Editor: Jane Loring. Assistant editor: Robert Parrish. Special effects: Vernon L. Walker. 123 minutes. Released: July 24. With Katharine Hepburn (Mary Stuart), Fredric March (Bothwell), Florence Eldridge (Elizabeth), Douglas Walton (Darnley), John Carradine (David Rizzio), Monte Blue (Messager), Jean Fenwick (Mary Seton), Robert Barrat (Morton), Gavin Muir (Leicester), Ian Keith (James Stuart Moray), Moroni Olsen (John Knox), Donald Crisp (Huntley), William Stack (Ruthven), Molly Lamont (Mary Livingston), Walter Byron (Sir Francis Walsingham), Ralph Forbes (Randolph), Alan Mowbray (Trockmorton), Frieda Inescort (Mary Beaton), David Torrence (Lindsay), Anita Colby (Mary Fleming), Lionel Belmore (English fisherman), Doris Lloyd (his wife), Bobby Watson (his son), Lionel Pape (Burghley), Ivan Simpson, Murray Kinnell, Lawrence Grant, Nigel DeBrulier, Barlowe Borland (judges), Alec Craig (Donal), Mary Gordon (nurse), Wilfred Lucas (Lexington), Leonard Mudie (Maitland), Brandon Hurst (Arian), D'Arcy Corrigan (Kirkcaldy), Frank Baker (Douglas), Cyril McLaglen (Faudoncide), Robert Warwick (Sir Francis Knellys), Earle Foxe (Duke of Kent), Wyndham Standing (sergeant), Gaston

Glass (Chatelard), Neil Fitzgerald (nobleman), Paul McAllister (Du Croche).

The reign of Mary, Queen of Scots, her rivalry with Elizabeth of England, her love affair with Bothwell, her final martyrdom. *'It did very well,' said Ford, 'though it was cut badly after I left.'*

1936 THE PLOUGH AND THE STARS (RKO Radio). Director: John Ford. Associate producers: Cliff Reid, Robert Sisk. Scenarist: Dudley Nichols, from play by Sean O'Casey. Photography: Joseph H. August. Art director: Van Nest Polglase. Music: Nathaniel Shilkret, Roy Webb. Editor: George Hively. 72 minutes. Released: December 26. With Barbara Stanwyck (Mora Clitheroe), Preston Foster (Jack Clitheroe), Barry Fitzgerald (Fluther Good), Dennis O'Dea (The Young Covey), Eileen Crowe (Bessie Burgess), Arthur Shields (Padraic Pearse), Erin O'Brien Moore (Rosie Redmond), Brandon Hurst (Sgt. Tinley), F. J. McCormick (Capt. Brennon), Una O'Conner (Maggie Corgan), Moroni Olsen (Gen. Connolly), J. M. Kerrigan (Peter Flynn), Neil Fitzgerald (Lt. Kangon), Bonita Granville (Mollser Gogan), Cyril McLaglen (Corporal Stoddart), Robert Homans (barman), Mary Gordon (first woman), Mary Quinn (second woman), Lionel Pape (the Englishman), Michael Fitzmaurice (ICA), Gaylord Pendleton (ICA), Doris Lloyd, D'Arcy Corrigan, Wesley Barry.

The story of a man and his wife told against the background of the Irish Rebellion in Easter Week, 1916.

1937 WEE WILLIE WINKIE (20th Century–Fox). Director: John Ford. Producer: Darryl F. Zanuck. Associate producer: Gene Markey. Scenarists: Ernest Pascal, Julian Josephson, from story by Rudyard Kipling. Photography: Arthur Miller. Set decorator: Thomas Little. Music: Louis Silvers. Editor: Walter Thompson. 99 minutes. Released (with tinted sequences): July 30. With Shirley Temple (Priscilla Williams), Victor McLaglen (Sgt MacDuff), C. Aubrey Smith (Col. Williams), June Lang (Joyce Williams), Michael Whalen (Lt. 'Coppy' Brandes), Cesar Romero (Khoda Khan), Constance Collier (Mrs. Allardyce), Douglas Scott (Mott), Gavin Muir (Capt. Bibberbeigh), Willie Fung (Mohammed Dihn), Brandon Hurst (Bagby), Lionel Pape (Major Allardyce), Clyde Cook (Pipe Major Sneath), Lauri Beatty (Elsi Allardyce), Lionel Braham (Major Gen. Hammond), Mary Forbes (Mrs. MacMonachie), Cyril McLaglen (Corporal Tummel), Pat Somerset (officer), Hector Sarno (conductor).

The adventures of a little girl at an 1890's British

Army post in Rajpore, India, where her grandfather is Colonel. Besides finding a husband for her widowed mother, making friends with a tough sergeant and softening the old colonel's overly strict regime, she manages to coax a notorious Indian rebel to sign a peace treaty.

1937 THE HURRICANE (Goldwyn–United Artists).

Director: John Ford. Producer: Samuel Goldwyn. Associate producer: Merritt Hulburd. Scenarist: Dudley Nichols, from novel by Charles Nordhoff, James Norman Hall, adapted by Oliver H. P. Garrett. Associate director: Stuart Heisler. Hurricane sequence: James Basevi. Photography: Bert Glennon, Archie Stout (second-unit). Art directors: Richard Day, Alex Golitzen. Set decorator: Julia Heron. Costumes: Omar Kiam. Music: Alfred Newman. Editor: Lloyd Nosler. Sound recording: Thomas Moulton. Assistant director: Wingate Smith. Exterior locations at Samoa. 102 minutes. Released: December 24. With Dorothy Lamour (Marama), Jon Hall (Terangi), Mary Astor (Mrs DeLaage), C. Aubrey Smith (Father Paul), Thomas Mitchell (Dr Kersaint), Raymond Massey (Mr DeLaage), John Carradine (guard), Jerome Cowan (Captain Nagle), Al Kikume (Chief Meheir), Kuulei DeClercq (Tita), Layne Tom, Jr. (Mako), Mamo Clark (Hitia), Movita Castenada (Arai), Reri (Reri), Francis Kaai (Tavi), Pauline Steele (Mata), Flora Hayes (Mama Rua), Mary Shaw (Marunga), Spencer Charters (judge), Roger Drake (captain of the guards), Inez Courtney (girl on boat), Paul Strader.

On a peaceful South Seas Island, a sadistic European governor sends an innocent native to jail for six months. Unable to stand the confinement, the youth escapes to join his new bride. When he is caught, the governor extends his sentence, but, instinctively, the native continues to break out—and each time his sentence is lengthened. During his final attempt, he kills a vicious guard, but before they can catch him, a terrible hurricane, as though sent by the gods, destroys the island and the helpless Europeans. *Ford: 'Jim Basevi conceived the hurricane itself and actually did all the mechanics. While he and I were shooting it, I gave Stu Heisler a second camera—you never knew what the hell would happen—and I said, "If the roof blows off or a sarong blows off or somebody falls down—get it." And as a matter of fact, I think he had quite a few shots in the picture.'* (The film received an Oscar for sound recording.)

1938 *The Adventures of Marco Polo* (Goldwyn–United Artists).

Director: Archie Mayo (and uncredited: John Ford). Producer: Samuel Goldwyn. Scenarist: Robert E. Sherwood, from story by N. A. Pogson. Photography: Rudolph Maté. Art director: Richard Day. Music: Alfred Newman. Special effects: James Basevi. 100 minutes. Released: April 15. With Gary Cooper, Sigrid Gurie, Basil Rathbone, George Barbier, Binnie Barnes, Ernest Truex, Alan Hale, H. B. Warner.

According to Ford, Mayo asked him to do some action scenes for the picture; his work includes a blizzard sequence and the scenes of Polo crossing the Himalayas.

1938 FOUR MEN AND A PRAYER (20th Century-Fox).

Director: John Ford. Producer: Darryl F. Zanuck. Associate producer: Kenneth Macgowan. Scenarists: Richard Sherman, Sonya Levien, Walter Ferris, from novel by David Garth. Photography: Ernest Palmer. Art directors: Bernard Herzbrun, Rudolph Sternad. Set decorator: Thomas Little. Music: Louis Silvers, Ernst Toch. Editor: Louis R. Loeffler. 85 minutes. Released: April 29. With Loretta Young (Lynn Cherrington), Richard Greene (Jeffrey Leigh), George Sanders (Wyatt Leigh), David Niven (Christopher Leigh), William Henry (Rodney Leigh), C. Aubrey Smith (Col. Loring Leigh), J. Edward Bromberg (General Torres), Alan Hale (Farnoy), John Carradine (Gen. Adolfo Arturo Sebastian), Reginald Denny (Douglas Loveland), Berton Churchill (Martin Cherrington), Claude King (Gen. Bryce), John Sutton (Capt. Drake), Barry Fitzgerald (Mulcahy), Cecil Cunningham (Pyer), Frank Baker (defense attorney), Frank Dawson (Mullins), Lina Basquette (Ah-Nee), William Stack (prosecuting attorney), Harry Hayden (Cherrington's secretary), Winter Hall (judge), Will Stanton (Cockney), John Spacey, C. Montague Shaw (lawyers), Lionel Pape (coroner), Brandon Hurst (jury foreman).

A British officer is unjustly disgraced and then murdered by gun runners in India. His four sons vow to avenge him and clear his name. They do.

1938 SUBMARINE PATROL (20th Century-Fox).

Director: John Ford. Producer: Darryl F. Zanuck. Associate producer: Gene Markey. Scenarists: Rian James, Darrell Ware, Jack Yellen, from novel, *The Splinter Fleet*, by John Milholland. Photography: Arthur Miller. Art directors: William Darling, Hans Peters. Set decorator: Thomas Little. Music director: Arthur Lange. Editor: Robert Simpson. 95 minutes. Released: November 25. With Richard Greene (Perry Townsend, III), Nancy Kelly (Susan Leeds), Preston Foster (Lt. John C. Drake), George Bancroft (Capt. Leeds), Slim Summerville (Ellsworth 'Spotts'

Ficketts), Joan Valerie (Anne), John Carradine (McAllison), Warren Hymer (Rocky Haggerty), Henry Armetta (Luigi), Douglas Fowley (Brett), J. Farrell McDonald (Quincannon), Dick Hogan (Johnny), Maxie Rosenbloom (Sgt Joe Duffy), Ward Bond (Olaf Swanson), Robert Lowery (Sparks), Charles Tannen (Kelly), George E. Stone (Irving), Moroni Olsen (Capt. Wilson), Jack Pennick (Guns McPeck), Elisha Cook, Jr. ('Professor' Pratt), Harry Strang (Grainger), Charles Trowbridge (Admiral Joseph Maitland), Victor Varconi (chaplain), Murray Alper (sailor), E. E. Clive.

A broken-down ship in the Splinter Fleet (whose job was searching out enemy submarines in World War I) is whipped into shape by a tough captain.

1939 STAGECOACH (Wanger-United Artists). Director-producer: John Ford. Executive producer: Walter Wanger. Scenarist: Dudley Nichols, from story, 'Stage to Lordsburg,' by Ernest Haycox. Photography: Bert Glennon. Art director: Alexander Toluboff. Set decorator: Wiard B. Ihnen. Costumes: Walter Plunkett. Music (adapted from 17 American folk tunes of early 1880's): Richard Hageman, W. Franke Harling, John Leipold, Leo Shuken, Louis Gruenberg. Editorial supervisor: Otho Lovering. Editors: Dorothy Spencer, Walter Reynolds. Assistant director: Wingate Smith. Filmed in Monument Valley and other locations in Arizona, Utah, California. 97 minutes. Released: March 2. With John Wayne (The Ringo Kid), Claire Trevor (Dallas), John Carradine (Hatfield), Thomas Mitchell (Dr Josiah Boone), Andy Devine (Buck), Donald Meek (Samuel Peacock), Louise Platt (Lucy Mallory), Tim Holt (Lt. Blanchard), George Bancroft (Sheriff Curly Wilcox), Berton Churchill (Henry Gatewood), Tom Tyler (Hank Plummer), Chris Pin Martin (Chris), Elvira Rios (Yakima, his wife), Francis Ford (Billy Pickett), Marga Daighton (Mrs Pickett), Kent Odell (Billy Pickett, Jr.), Yakima Canutt, Chief Big Tree (stuntmen), Harry Tenbrook (telegraph operator), Jack Pennick (Jerry, barman), Paul McVey (Express Agent), Cornelius Keefe (Capt. Whitney), Florence Lake (Mrs Nancy Whitney), Louis Mason (Sheriff), Brenda Fowler (Mrs Gatewood), Walter McGrail (Capt. Sickel), Joseph Rickson (Luke Plummer), Vester Pegg (Ike Plummer), William Hoffer (sergeant), Bryant Washburn (Capt. Simmons), Nora Cecil (Dr Boone's housekeeper), Helen Gibson, Dorothy Annleby (dancing girls), Buddy Roosevelt, Bill Cody (ranchers), Chief White Horse (Indian chief), Duke Lee (Sheriff of Lordsburg), Mary Kathleen Walker (Lucy's baby), Ed Brady, Steve Clemente, Theodore Larch, Fritzi Brunette, Leonard Trainor, Chris Phillips, Tex Driscoll, Teddy Billings, John Eckert, Al Lee, Jack Mohr, Patsy

Doyle, Wiggie Blowne, Margaret Smith.

1884. A group of misfits—of one kind or another—cross the New Mexico Territory in a stagecoach, threatened and finally attacked by Apaches. *Probably Ford's most famous western, and the first to be shot in Monument Valley. The New York Film Critics gave him their Best Director award; and Oscars went to the composers and to Thomas Mitchell as best supporting actor. Footage from the chase has been used in at least two B westerns: I Killed Geronimo, 1950, and Laramie Mountains, 1952. The film was remade, abominably, in 1966.)*

1939 YOUNG MR LINCOLN (Cosmopolitan-20th Century-Fox). Director: John Ford. Executive producer: Darryl F. Zanuck. Producer: Kenneth Macgowan. Scenarist: Lamar Trotti, based on life of Abraham Lincoln. Photography: Bert Glennon. Art directors: Richard Day, Mark Lee Kirk. Set decorator: Thomas Little. Music: Alfred Newman. Editor: Walter Thompson. Sound effects editor: Robert Parrish. 101 minutes. Released: June 9. With Henry Fonda (Abraham Lincoln), Alice Brady (Abigail Clay), Marjorie Weaver (Mary Todd), Dorris Bowdon (Hannah Clay), Eddie Collins (Efe Turner), Pauline Moore (Ann Rutledge), Richard Cromwell (Matt Clay), Ward Bond (John Palmer Cass), Donald Meek (John Felder), Spencer Charters (Judge Herbert A. Bell), Eddie Quillan (Adam Clay), Judith Dickens (Carrie Sue), Milburn Stone (Stephen A. Douglas), Cliff Clark (Sheriff Billings), Robert Lowery (juror), Charles Tannen (Ninian Edwards), Francis Ford (Sam Boone), Fred Kohler, Jr. (Scrub White), Kay Linaker (Mrs Edwards), Russell Simpson (Woolridge), Charles Halton (Hawthorne), Edwin Maxwell (John T. Stuart), Robert Homans (Mr Clay), Jack Kelly (Matt Clay, as child), Dicky Jones (Adam Clay, as child), Harry Tyler (hairdresser), Louis Mason (court clerk), Jack Pennick (juror), Clarence Wilson, Elizabeth Jones.

The early life of Abe Lincoln, his tragic love for Ann Rutledge, his decision to become a lawyer and his first trial, in which he defends two brothers on a murder charge and proves them innocent.

1939 DRUMS ALONG THE MOHAWK (20th Century-Fox). Director: John Ford. Executive producer: Darryl F. Zanuck. Producer: Raymond Griffith. Scenarists: Lamar Trotti, Sonya Levien and (uncredited) William Faulkner, from novel by Walter D. Edmonds. Photography (in color): Bert Glennon, Ray Rennahan. Art directors: Richard Day, Mark Lee Kirk. Set decorator: Thomas Little. Music:

Alfred Newman. Editor: Robert Simpson. Sound effects editor: Robert Parrish. 103 minutes. Released: November 3. With Claudette Colbert (Lana Borst Martin), Henry Fonda (Gilbert Martin), Edna May Oliver (Mrs McKlennan), Eddie Collins (Christian Reall), John Carradine (Caldwell), Dorris Bowdon (Mary Reall), Jessie Ralph (Mrs Weaver), Arthur Shields (Father Rosenkranz), Robert Lowery (John Weaver), Roger Imhof (General Nicholas Herkimer), Francis Ford (Joe Boleo), Ward Bond (Adam Hartmann), Kay Linaker (Mrs Demooth), Russell Simpson (Dr Petry), Chief Big Tree (Blue Back), Spencer Charters (Fisk, innkeeper), Arthur Aylesworth (George), Si Jenks (Jacobs), Jack Pennick (Amos), Charles Tannen (Robert Johnson), Paul McVey (Capt. Mark Demooth), Elizabeth Jones (Mrs Reall), Lionel Pape (General), Clarence Wilson (Paymaster), Edwin Maxwell (pastor), Clara Blandick (Mrs Borst), Beulah Hall Jones (Daisy), Robert Greig (Mr Borst), Mae Marsh.

The experiences of a young couple in the Mohawk Valley before and during the Revolutionary War. *Ford's first film in color. Footage used in other films, notably* Mohawk, *in* 1956.

1940 THE GRAPES OF WRATH (20th Century-Fox). Director: John Ford. Producer: Darryl F. Zanuck. Associate producer-scenarist: Nunnally Johnson, from novel by John Steinbeck. Photography: Gregg Toland. Art directors: Richard Day, Mark Lee Kirk. Set decorator: Thomas Little. Music: Alfred Newman. Song, 'Red River Valley,' played on accordion by Dan Borzage. Second-unit director: Otto Brower. Editor: Robert Simpson. Sound: George Leverett, Roger Heman. Sound effects editor: Robert Parrish. Assistant director: Edward O'Fearna. 129 minutes. Released: March 15. With Henry Fonda (Tom Joad), Jane Darwell (Ma Joad), John Carradine (Casey), Charley Grapewin (Grampa Joad), Dorris Bowdon (Rosasharn), Russell Simpson (Pa Joad), O. Z. Whitehead (Al), John Qualen (Muley), Eddie Quillan (Connie), Zeffie Tilbury (Grandma Joad), Frank Sully (Noah), Frank Darien (Uncle John), Darryl Hickman (Winfield), Shirley Mills (Ruth Joad), Grant Mitchell (guardian), Ward Bond (policeman), Frank Faylen (Tim), Joe Sawyer (accountant), Harry Tyler (Bert), Charles B. Middleton (conductor), John Arledge (Davis), Hollis Jewell (Muley's son), Paul Guilfoyle (Floyd), Charles D. Brown (Wilkie), Roger Imhof (Thomas), William Pawley (Bill), Arthur Aylesworth (father), Charles Tannen (Joe), Selmar Jackson (inspector), Eddie C. Waller (proprietor), David Hughes (Frank), Cliff Clark (townsman), Adrian Morris (agent), Robert Homans (Spencer), Irving Bacon (conductor),

Kitty McHugh (Mae), Mae Marsh, Francis Ford, Jack Pennick.

The odyssey of the Joads, a family of Oakies forced off their land in the dustbowl of the 30's. *Ford and Jane Darwell received Oscars and Ford won the New York Film Critics Award for his work on this and* The Long Voyage Home.

1940 THE LONG VOYAGE HOME (Wanger-United Artists). Director: John Ford. Producer: Walter Wanger. Scenarist: Dudley Nichols, from one-act plays, 'The Moon of the Caribbees,' 'In the Zone,' 'Bound East for Cardiff,' 'The Long Voyage Home,' by Eugene O'Neill. Photography: Gregg Toland. Art director: James Basevi. Set decorator: Julia Heron. Music: Richard Hageman. Editor: Sherman Todd. Sound editor: Robert Parrish. Special effects: Ray Binger, R. T. Layton. 105 minutes. Released: October 8. With Thomas Mitchell (Aloysius Driscoll), John Wayne (Ole Olsen), Ian Hunter (Thomas Fenwick, 'Smitty'), Barry Fitzgerald (Cocky), Wilfred Lawson (Captain), Mildred Natwick (Freda), John Qualen (Axel Swanson), Ward Bond (Yank), Joe Sawyer (Davis), Arthur Shields (Donkeyman), J. M. Kerrigan (Crimp), David Hughes (Scotty), Billy Bevan (Joe), Cyril McLaglen (Mate), Robert E. Perry (Paddy), Jack Pennick (Johnny Bergman), Constantin Frenke (Narvey), Constantin Romanoff (Big Frank), Dan Borzage (Tim), Harry Tenbrook (Max), Douglas Walton (Second Lieutenant), Raphaela Ottiano (Daughter of the Tropics), Carmen Morales, Carmen d'Antonio (girls in canoe), Harry Woods (the Admiral's sailor), Edgar 'Blue' Washington, Lionel Pape, Jane Crowley, Maureen Roden-Ryan.

Each man on the Glencairn looks forward in his own way to the end of the voyage, but, as always, they find the land as disappointing as the sea and all but one sign on for another run. *O'Neill's favorite among the films made of his work, and the only one he looked at periodically.*

1941 TOBACCO ROAD (20th Century-Fox). Director: John Ford. Producer: Darryl F. Zanuck. Associate producers: Jack Kirkland, Harry H. Oshrin. Scenarist: Nunnally Johnson, from play by Kirkland and novel by Erskine Caldwell. Photography: Arthur C. Miller. Art directors: Richard Day, James Basevi. Set decorator: Thomas Little. Music: David Buttolph. Editor: Barbara McLean. Sound effects editor: Robert Parrish. 84 minutes. Released: February 20. With Charley Grapewin (Jeeter Lester), Marjorie Rambeau (Sister Bessie), Gene Tierney (Ellie May Lester), William Tracy (Dude Lester), Elizabeth Patterson

(Ada Lester), Dana Andrews (Dr Tim), Slim Summerville (Henry Peabody), Ward Bond (Lov Bensey), Grant Mitchell (George Payne), Zeffie Tilbury (Grandma Lester), Russell Simpson (Sheriff), Spencer Charters (employee), Irving Bacon (teller), Harry Tyler (auto salesman), George Chandler (employee), Charles Halton (Mayor), Jack Pennick (Deputy Sheriff), Dorothy Adams (Payne's secretary), Francis Ford (vagabond).

The futile lives of a decadent poor-white Georgia family.

1941 SEX HYGIENE (Audio Productions–U.S. Army). Director: John Ford   Producer: Darryl F. Zanuck. Photographer: George Barnes. Editor: Gene Fowler, Jr. 30 minutes. With Charles Trowbridge.

An Army training film on the dangers of, and ways to prevent, venereal disease.

1941 HOW GREEN WAS MY VALLEY (20th Century-Fox). Director: John Ford. Producer: Darryl F. Zanuck. Scenarist: Philip Dunne, from novel by Richard Llewellyn. Photography: Arthur Miller. Art directors: Richard Day, Nathan Juran. Set decorator: Thomas Little. Costumes: Gwen Wakeling. Music: Alfred Newman. Choral effects: Eisteddfod Singers of Wales. Editor: James B. Clark. Narrator: Rhys Williams. 118 minutes. Released: December. With Walter Pidgeon (Mr Gruffydd), Maureen O'Hara (Angharad Morgan), Donald Crisp (Mr Morgan), Anna Lee (Bronwen Morgan), Roddy McDowall (Huw Morgan), John Loder (Ianto Morgan), Sara Allgood (Mrs Beth Morgan), Barry Fitzgerald (Cyfartha), Patrick Knowles (Ivor Morgan), The Welsh Singers (singers), Morton Lowery (Mr. Jonas), Arthur Shields (Mr Parry), Ann Todd (Ceiwen), Frederick Worlock (Dr Richards), Richard Fraser (Davy Morgan), Evan S. Evans (Gwinlyn), James Monks (Owen Morgan), Rhys Williams (Dai Bando), Lionel Pape (Old Evans), Ethel Griffies (Mrs Nicholas), Marten Lamont (Jestyn Evans), Mae Marsh (miner's wife), Louis Jean Heydt (miner), Denis Hoey (Motschell), Tudor Williams (singer), Clifford Severn, Eve March.

The slow and tragic disintegration of a Welsh mining family and of the Valley in which they lived. (*Oscars for Ford, Best Picture, Donald Crisp, Arthur Miller, the art directors; and Ford's fourth award from the New York Film Critics.*)

When he had completed *How Green Was My Valley*, Ford went on active duty in the Navy. He was appointed Chief of the Field Photographic Branch, a unit of the O.S.S. (Office of Strategic Services) with offices in Paris and London. Among those he took with him were Gregg Toland, Joseph Walker, Budd Schulberg, Garson Kanin, Daniel Fuchs, Claude Dauphin, Robert Parrish, Jack Pennick, Ray Kellogg, Harold Wenstrom. 'Our job,' Ford once told a newsman, 'was to photograph, both for the Records and for intelligence assessment, the work of guerrillas, saboteurs, Resistance outfits. . . . Besides this, there were special assignments.'

1942 THE BATTLE OF MIDWAY (U.S. Navy–20th Century-Fox). Director-photographer: Lt. Commander John Ford, U.S.N.R. Narration written by Ford, Dudley Nichols, James Kevin McGuinness. Additional photography: Jack McKenzie. Music: Alfred Newman. Editors: Ford, Robert Parrish. 20 minutes. Released (in color): September. With the voices of Henry Fonda, Jane Darwell, Donald Crisp.

America's first war documentary (it received the Academy Award as such), filmed during the actual battle. Although he was wounded in the first attack, Ford continued to photograph the events himself.

1942 TORPEDO SQUADRON (U.S. Navy). Director: Lt. Commander John Ford, U.S.N.R. 8 minutes in colour.

Just before the battle of Midway, a photographer in Ford's unit took some 16 mm. colour footage of life on a PT Boat—Torpedo Squadron 8. When all but one man in this squadron were killed during the battle, Ford had the footage edited and reduced to an 8 mm. film to be seen only by the families of the dead boys. Prints were delivered to them by personal envoys (such as Joe August) and the film was never used for any other purpose.

1943 DECEMBER 7TH (U.S. Navy). Directors: Lt. Gregg Toland, U.S.N.R., Lt. Commander John Ford, U.S.N.R. Photography: Toland. Second-unit director: James C. Havens, U.S.M.C. Music: Alfred Newman. Editor: Robert Parrish. 20 minutes.

An Academy Award-winning documentary about the bombing of Pearl Harbor. According to Ford, his unit arrived about six days after the attack. 'Gregg Toland directed that,' he says. 'I helped him along, I was there, but Gregg was in charge of it.'

1943 WE SAIL AT MIDNIGHT (Crown Film Unit–U.S. Navy). Director: Lt. Commander John Ford, U.S.N.R. Narration written by Clifford Odets. Music: Richard

Addinsell. 20 minutes. Released: July.

A documentary about the hazards of getting merchant ships through combat zones. *This and other documentaries were composed of footage, the shooting of which Ford supervised, but, according to him, only the first couple were actually completed by him; in most cases, the material was turned over to others who then cut it into a finished picture.*

1943 *The Last Outlaw* (Unrealized project).

Ford planned a remake of the 1919 two-reeler to be his first feature when the war was over; he worked on the script, adding characters and altering the ending, and preliminary negotiations were conducted with Herbert J. Yates of Republic Pictures. The film was to star Ford's old friend, Harry Carey.

After the war, Ford and his group began to prepare a film for the Nuremberg Trials that would have run seven or eight hours. There was to have been a section on each of the major war criminals, and the greatest part of the work was in going through hundreds of thousands of feet of film looking for clips that could serve as evidence against the accused. When Gen. Donovan was ordered elsewhere, the project was dropped.

1945 THEY WERE EXPENDABLE (Metro-Goldwyn-Mayer).

Director-producer: John Ford. Associate producer: Cliff Reid. Scenarist: Frank W. Wead, from book by William L. White. Photography: Joseph H. August. Art directors: Cedric Gibbons, Malcolm F. Brown. Set decorators: Edwin B. Willis, Ralph S. Hurst. Music: Herbert Stothart. Editors: Frank E. Hull, Douglas Biggs. Second-unit director: James C. Havens (rear projection plates by Robert Montgomery). Assistant director: Edward O'Fearna. 136 minutes. Released: December 20. With Robert Montgomery (Lt. John Brickley), John Wayne (Lt. Rusty Ryan), Donna Reed (Lt. Sandy Davis), Jack Holt (General Martin), Ward Bond (Boots Mulcahey), Louis Jean Heydt (Ohio, flyer in hospital), Marshall Thompson (Snake Gardner), Russell Simpson (Dad, chief of shipyard), Leon Ames (Major Morton), Paul Langton (Andy Andrews), Arthur Walsh (Jones), Donald Curtis (Shorty Long), Cameron Mitchell (George Cross), Jeff York (Tony Aiken), Murray Alper (Slug Mahan), Harry Tenbrook (Larsen), Jack Pennick (Doc Charlie), Charles Trowbridge (Admiral Blackwell), Robert Barrat (General Douglas MacArthur), Bruce Kellogg (Tomkins), Tim Murdock (Ens. Brown), Vernon Steele (doctor), Alex Havier (Benny), Eve March (nurse), Pedro de Cordoba (priest), Trina Lowe (Gardner's girlfriend), Pacita Tod-Tod (nightclub singer), William B. Davidson (hotel manager), Robert Emmett O'Conner (Silver Dollar bartender), Max Ong (Mayor of Cebu), Bill Wilkerson (Sgt. Smith), John Carlyle (Lt. James), Phillip Ahn (orderly), Betty Blythe (officer's wife), Kermit Maynard (airport officer),

Stubby Kruger, Sammy Stein, Michael Kirby, Blake Edwards (boat crew), Wallace Ford, Tom Tyler.

The story of the man who pioneered the use of the PT Boat in combat, told against the background of America's worst defeat, in the Philippines. *Ford used his salary from this film to build a recreation centre, 'The Farm,' for Field Photographic Branch veterans. Battle footage used in* Malaya, *1950* (Richard Thorp, M-G-M).

1946 MY DARLING CLEMENTINE (20th Century-Fox).

Director: John Ford. Producer: Samuel G. Engel. Scenarists: Engel, Winston Miller, from story by Sam Hellman, based on book, *Wyatt Earp, Frontier Marshal,* by Stuart N. Lake. Photography: Joseph P. MacDonald. Art directors: James Basevi, Lyle R. Wheeler. Set decorators: Thomas Little, Fred J. Rode. Costumes: Rene Hubert. Music: Cyril J. Mockridge. Editor: Dorothy Spencer. Assistant director: William Eckhardt. Exteriors filmed in Monument Valley. 97 minutes. Released: November. With Henry Fonda (Wyatt Earp), Linda Darnell (Chihuahua), Victor Mature (Doc John Holliday), Walter Brennan (Old Man Clanton), Tim Holt (Virgil Earp), Ward Bond (Morgan Earp), Cathy Downs (Clementine Carter), Alan Mowbray (Granville Thorndyke), John Ireland (Billy Clanton), Grant Withers (Ike Clanton), Roy Roberts (Mayor), Jane Darwell (Kate Nelson), Russell Simpson (John Simpson), Francis Ford (Dad, old soldier), J. Farrell McDonald (Mac, barman), Don Garner (James Earp), Ben Hall (barber), Arthur Walsh (hotel clerk), Jack Pennick, Robert Adler (stagecoach drivers), Louis Mercier (Francois), Mickey Simpson (Sam Clanton), Fred Libby (Phin Clanton), Harry Woods (Luke), Charles Stevens (Indian troublemaker), William B. Davidson (Oriental saloon owner), Earle Foxe (gambler), Aleth 'Speed' Hansen (guitarist), Danny Borzage (accordionist), Frank Conlan (pianist), Don Barclay (opera house owner), Mae Marsh.

The story of Wyatt Earp's Tombstone days and his relationship with the consumptive Doc Holliday. *A remake, considerably altered, of Allan Dwan's 1939* Frontier Marshal; *the same basic story has since been used in numerous films, most expensively in* Gunfight at the O.K. Corral, *1957.*

1947 THE FUGITIVE (Argosy Pictures-RKO Radio).

Director: John Ford. Producers: Ford, Merian C. Cooper. Associate producer: Emilio Fernandez. Scenarist: Dudley Nichols, from novel, *The Labyrinthine Ways* (or *The Power and the Glory*), by Graham Greene. Photography: Gabriel Figueroa. Art director: Alfred Ybarra. Set decorator: Manuel Parra. Music: Richard Hageman. Editor: Jack Murray. Executive assistant: Jack Pennick. Directorial assistant: Melchor Ferrer. Assistant director: Jesse Hibbs. Filmed in 47 days on locations in Mexico and at Churubusco Studios, Mexico City. 104 minutes. Released:

November 3. With Henry Fonda (The Fugitive), Dolores Del Rio (Mexican woman), Pedro Armendariz (Police Lieutenant), Ward Bond (El Gringo), Leo Carrillo (Chief of Police,) J. Carroll Naish (police spy), Robert Armstrong (Police Sergeant), John Qualen (Doctor), Fortunio Bonanova (Governor's cousin), Chris Pin Martin (organ player), Miguel Inclan (hostage), Fernando Fernandez (singer), Jose I. Torvay (a Mexican), Melchor Ferrer.

The flight of a priest through a police state, paralleled with that of a wanted criminal.

1947 *The Family* (Unrealized project). Ford had planned to film Nina Federova's 1940 novel (which had won the Atlantic Monthly Prize) with John Wayne and Ethel Barrymore in the cast. The book deals with a family of White Russians who are exiled to China after the Revolution. In an interview at the time, Ford said, 'It's simply the story of the disintegration of a family after it has been unrooted.'

1948 FORT APACHE (Argosy Pictures-RKO Radio). Director: John Ford. Producers: Ford, Merian C. Cooper. Scenarist: Frank S. Nugent, from story, 'Massacre,' by James Warner Bellah. Photography: Archie Stout, William Clothier (second-unit). Art director: James Basevi. Set decorator: Joe Kish. Music: Richard Hageman. Second-unit director: Cliff Lyons. Production manager: Bernard McEveety. Assistant directors: Lowell Farrell, Jack Pennick. Filmed in 45 days on locations in Utah and in Monument Valley. 127 minutes. Released: March 9. With John Wayne (Capt. Kirby York), Henry Fonda (Lt. Col. Owen Thursday), Shirley Temple (Philadelphia Thursday), John Agar (Lt. Michael O'Rourke), Ward Bond (Sgt. Major O'Rourke), George O'Brien (Captain Sam Collingwood), Victor McLaglen (Sgt Mulcahy), Pedro Armendariz (Sgt Beaufort), Anna Lee (Mrs Collingwood), Irene Rich (Mrs O'Rourke), Guy Kibbee (Dr Wilkens), Grant Withers (Silas Meacham), Miguel Inclan (Cochise), Jack Pennick (Sgt Schattuck), Mae Marsh (Mrs Gates), Dick Foran (Sgt Quincannon), Frank Ferguson (newspaperman), Francis Ford (bartender), Ray Hyke (Gates), Movita Castenada (Guadalupe), Hank Worden (Southern recruit) Harry Tenbrook (courier), Mary Gordon (woman in stagecoach).

The first in Ford's (unofficial) Cavalry trilogy, about an arrogant Lt. Col. who leads his men into an Apache massacre.

1948 3 GODFATHERS (Argosy Pictures-Metro-Goldwyn-Mayer).
Director: John Ford. Producers: Ford, Merian C. Cooper. Scenarists: Laurence Stallings, Frank S. Nugent, from story by Peter B. Kyne. Photography

138

(in colour): Winton C. Hoch, Charles P. Boyle (second unit). Art director: James Basevi. Set decorator: Joe Kish. Music: Richard Hageman. Editor: Jack Murray. Production manager: Lowell Farrell. Assistant directors: Wingate Smith, Edward O'Fearna. Filmed in 32 days on locations in the Mojave Desert. 106 minutes. Released: December 1. With John Wayne (Robert Marmaduke Sangster Hightower), Pedro Armendariz (Pedro Roca Fuerte), Harry Carey, Jr. (William Kearney, 'The Abilene Kid'), Ward Bond (Perley 'Buck' Sweet), Mildred Natwick (mother), Charles Halton (Mr Latham), Jane Darwell (Miss Florie), Mae Marsh (Mrs Perley Sweet), Guy Kibbee (judge), Dorothy Ford (Ruby Latham), Ben Johnson, Michael Dugan, Don Summers (patrolmen), Fred Libby (Deputy Sheriff), Hank Worden (Deputy Sheriff), Jack Pennick (Luke, train conductor), Francis Ford (drunk), Ruth Clifford (woman in bar).

A remake of Ford's *Marked Men*, dedicated to the star of that film who had died the year before: 'To the memory of Harry Carey—bright star of the early western sky.'

1949 *Mighty Joe Young* (Argosy Pictures-RKO Radio). Director: Ernest B. Schoedsack. Producers: John Ford, Merian C. Cooper. Scenarist: Ruth Rose, from story by Cooper. Photography: J. Roy Hunt. Art director: James Basevi. 94 minutes. Released: July 30. With Terry Moore, Ben Johnson, Robert Armstrong, Frank McHugh, Regis Toomey.

Ford: 'I had nothing to do with it.'

1949 SHE WORE A YELLOW RIBBON (Argosy Pictures-RKO Radio).
Director: John Ford. Producers: Ford, Merian C. Cooper. Associate producer: Lowell Farrell. Scenarists: Frank S. Nugent, Laurence Stallings, from story, 'War Party,' by James Warner Bellah. Photography (in colour): Winton C. Hoch, Charles P. Boyle (second-unit). Art director: James Basevi. Set decorator: Joe Kish. Music: Richard Hageman. Editor: Jack Murray. Assistant editor: Barbara Ford. Second-unit director: Cliff Lyons. Assistant directors: Wingate Smith, Edward O'Fearna. Filmed in 31 days on locations in Monument Valley. 103 minutes. Released: October 22. With John Wayne (Capt. Nathan Brittles), Joanne Dru (Olivia), John Agar (Lt. Flint Cohill), Ben Johnson (Sgt Tyree), Harry Carey, Jr. (Lt. Pennell), Victor McLaglen (Sgt Quincannon), Mildred Natwick (Mrs Allshard), George O'Brien (Maj. MacAllshard), Arthur Shields (Dr O'Laughlin), Francis Ford (barman), Harry Woods (Karl Rynders), Chief Big Tree (Pony That Walks), Noble Johnson (Red Shirt), Cliff Lyons (Trooper Cliff),

Tom Tyler (Quayne), Michael Dugan (Hochbauer), Mickey Simpson (Wagner), Fred Graham (Hench), Frank McGrath (trumpeter), Don Summers (Jenkins), Fred Libby (Colonel Krumrein), Jack Pennick (Sgt. Major), Billy Jones (courier), Bill Gettinger (officer), Fred Kennedy (Badger), Rudy Bowman (Pvt. Smith), Post Park (officer), Ray Hyke (McCarthy), Lee Bradley (interpreter), Chief Sky Eagle, Dan White.

The second in the cavalry trilogy, about an ageing captain's last mission before retirement. (*Oscar to Hoch for the photography.*)

1949 *Pinky* (20th Century–Fox).
Director: Elia Kazan (and uncredited: John Ford). Producer: Darryl F. Zanuck. Scenarists: Philip Dunne, Dudley Nichols, from novel, *Quality*, by Cid Ricketts Sumner. Photography: Joseph MacDonald. Music: Alfred Newman. Assistant director: Wingate Smith. 102 minutes. Released: November. With Jeanne Crain, Ethel Barrymore, Ethel Waters, William Lundigan, Basil Ruysdael.

The story of a Negro girl who passed for white. Ford: '*I prepared it and worked one day on it before I got ill. I forget what I shot.*' (*Only Pinky's return to her home at the beginning looks particularly Fordian.*)

1950 WHEN WILLIE COMES MARCHING HOME (20th Century–Fox).
Director: John Ford. Producer: Fred Kohlmar. Scenarists: Mary Loos, Richard Sale, from story, 'When Leo Comes Marching Home,' by Sy Gomberg. Photography: Leo Tover. Art directors: Lyle R. Wheeler, Chester Gore. Set decorators: Thomas Little, Bruce MacDonald. Music: Alfred Newman. Editor: James B. Clark. Assistant director: Wingate Smith. 82 minutes. Released: February. With Dan Dailey (Bill Kluggs), Corinne Calvet (Yvonne), Colleen Townsend (Marge Fettles), William Demarest (Herman Kluggs), Jame Lydon (Charles Fettles), Lloyd Corrigan (Mayor Adams), Evelyn Varden (Gertrude Kluggs), Kenny Williams (musician), Lee Clark (musician), Charles Halton (Mr Fettles), Mae Marsh (Mrs Fettles), Jack Pennick (Sergeant-Instructor), Mickey Simpson (M.P. Kerrigan), Frank Pershing (Major Bickford), Don Summers (M.P. Sherve), Gil Herman (Lt. Commander Crown), Peter Ortiz (Pierre), Luis Alberni (barman), John Shulick (pilot), Clarke Gordon, Robin Hughes (Marine officers), Cecil Weston (Mrs Barnes), Harry Tenbrook (Joe, taxi driver), Russ Clark (Sgt Wilson), George Spaulding (Judge Tate), James Eagle (reporter), Harry Strang (sergeant), George Magrill (Chief Petty Officer), Hank Worden (choir leader), John McKee (pilot), Larry Keating (Gen. G. Reeding), Dan Riss (Gen. Adams), Robert Einer (Lt. Bagley), Russ Conway

(Maj. J. A. White), Whit Bissell (Lt. Handley), Ann Codee (French instructor), Ray Hyke (Maj. Crawford), Gene Collins (Andy), James Flavin (Gen. Brevort), David McMahon (Col. Ainsley), Charles Trowbridge (Gen. Merrill), Kenneth Tobey (Lt. K. Geiger), Maj. Sam Harris (hospital patient), Alberto Morin, Louis Mercier (Resistance fighters), Paul Harvey (officer), James Waters, Ken Lynch.

Sgt. Kluggs is the first man in his hometown to enter the Army in World War II and he gets stationed—in his hometown. His pleas to go overseas go unanswered, until finally he is sent on a dangerous top secret mission behind the lines in France. When he returns only four days have passed and no one believes he ever left. (Actually a look at the Army by a Navy man.)

1950 WAGON MASTER (Argosy Pictures–RKO Radio).
Director: John Ford. Producers: Ford, Merian C. Cooper. Associate producer: Lowell Farrell. Writers: Frank S. Nugent, Patrick Ford. Photography: Bert Glennon, Archie Stout (second-unit). Art director: James Basevi. Set decorator: Joe Kish. Music: Richard Hageman. Songs, 'Wagons West,' 'Rollin' Shadows in the Dust,' 'Song of the Wagon Master,' 'Chuck-A-Walla-Swing,' by Stan Jones, sung by The Sons of the Pioneers. Editor: Jack Murray. Assistant editor: Barbara Ford. Second-unit director: Cliff Lyons. Assistant director: Wingate Smith. Filmed in Monument Valley and in Professor Valley, Utah. 86 minutes. Released: April 19. With Ben Johnson (Travis Blue), Harry Carey, Jr. (Sandy Owens), Joanne Dru (Denver), Ward Bond (Elder Wiggs), Charles Kemper (Uncle Shiloh Clegg), Alan Mowbray (Dr A. Locksley Hall), Jane Darwell (Sister Ledeyard), Ruth Clifford (Fleuretty Phyffe), Russell Simpson (Adam Perkins), Kathleen O'Malley (Prudence Perkins), James Arness (Floyd Clegg), Fred Libby (Reese Clegg), Hank Worden (Luke Clegg), Mickey Simpson (Jesse Clegg), Francis Ford (Mr. Peachtree), Cliff Lyons (Sheriff of Crystal City), Don Summers (Sam Jenkins), Movita Castenada (young Navajo girl), Jim Thorpe (Navajo), Chuck Hayward (Jackson).

A Mormon wagon train, guided by two young horse traders, is menaced by Indians and outlaws as it makes its way across the country to Utah in the 1870's.

1950 RIO GRANDE (Argosy Pictures–Republic).
Director: John Ford. Producers: Ford, Merian C. Cooper. Scenarist: James Kevin McGuinness, from story, 'Mission With No Record,' by James Warner Bellah. Photography: Bert Glennon, Archie Stout (second-unit). Art director: Frank Hotaling. Set

decorators: John McCarthy, Jr., Charles Thompson. Music: Victor Young. Songs, sung by The Sons of the Pioneers: 'My Gal Is Purple,' 'Footsore Cavalry,' 'Yellow Stripes,' by Stan Jones; 'Aha, San Antone,' by Dale Evans; 'Cattle Call,' by Tex Owens; and 'Erie Canal,' 'I'll Take You Home Again, Kathleen,' 'Down by the Glen Side,' 'You're in the Army Now'. Editor: Jack Murray. Assistant editor: Barbara Ford. Second-unit director: Cliff Lyons. 105 minutes. Released: November 15. With John Wayne (Lt. Col. Kirby Yorke), Maureen O'Hara (Mrs Yorke), Ben Johnson (Trooper Tyree), Claude Jarman, Jr. (Trooper Jeff Yorke), Harry Carey, Jr. (Trooper Daniel Boone), Chill Wills (Dr Wilkins), J. Carroll Naish (Gen. Philip Sheridan), Victor McLaglen (Sgt Quincannon), Grant Withers (Deputy Marshal), Peter Ortiz (Capt. St Jacques), Steve Pendleton (Capt. Prescott), Karolyn Grimes (Margaret Mary), Alberto Morin (lieutenant), Stan Jones (sergeant), Fred Kennedy (Heinze), Jack Pennick, Pat Wayne, Chuck Roberson, The Sons of the Pioneers (regimental singers): Ken Curtis, Hugh Farr, Karl Farr, Lloyd Perryman, Shug Fisher, Tommy Doss.

Last of the cavalry trilogy, about a colonel, his wife and son—estranged since the Civil War—who are drawn together during an episode in the Apache wars near the Mexican Border.

In 1951, John Wayne produced and Budd Boetticher directed *The Bullfighter and the Lady*. Ford: 'I like Budd very much. The picture was too long and he asked me to come in and help him cut it, so I did.'

1951 THIS IS KOREA! (U.S. Navy–Republic). Director: Rear Admiral John Ford, U.S.N.R. 50 minutes. Released (in color): August 10. With the voices of John Ireland, others.

A documentary picture of what the war was like in Korea.

1952 WHAT PRICE GLORY (20th Century–Fox). Director: John Ford. Producer: Sol C. Siegel. Scenarists: Phoebe and Henry Ephron, from play by Maxwell Anderson, Laurence Stallings. Photography (in color): Joseph MacDonald. Art directors: Lyle R. Wheeler, George W. Davis. Set decorators: Thomas Little, Stuart A. Reiss. Music: Alfred Newman. Song, 'My Love, My Life,' by Jay Livingston, Roy Evans. Editor: Dorothy Spencer. 111 minutes. Released: August. With James Cagney (Capt. Flagg), Corinne Calvet (Charmaine), Dan Dailey (Sgt Quirt), William Demarest (Corporal Kiper), Craig Hill (Lt. Aldrich), Robert Wagner (Lewisohn), Marisa Pavan (Nicole Bouchard), Casey Adams (Lt. Moore),

James Gleason (Gen. Cokely), Wally Vernon (Lipinsky), Henry Letondal (Cognac Pete), Fred Libby (Lt. Schmidt), Ray Hyke (Mulcahy), Paul Fix (Gowdy), James Lilburn (young soldier), Henry Morgan (Morgan), Dan Borzage (Gilbert), Bill Henry (Holsen), Henry 'Bomber' Kulkovich (company cook), Jack Pennick (Ferguson), Ann Codee (nun), Stanley Johnson (Lt. Cunningham), Tom Tyler (Capt. Davis), Olga Andre (Sister Clotilde), Barry Norton (priest), Luis Alberni (the great uncle), Torben Meyer (mayor), Alfred Zeisler (English colonel), George Bruggeman (English lieutenant), Scott Forbes (Lt. Bennett), Sean McClory (Lt. Austin), Charles FitzSimmons (Capt. Wickham), Louis Mercier (Bouchard), Mickey Simpson (M.P.), Peter Ortiz, Paul Guilfoyle.

The adventures of Capt. Flagg and Sgt Quirt in a French village during World War I. *A remake of Raoul Walsh's famous 1926 film.*

1952 THE QUIET MAN (Argosy Pictures–Republic). Director: John Ford. Producers: Ford, Merian C. Cooper. Scenarist: Frank S. Nugent, from story by Maurice Walsh. Photography (in color): Winton C. Hoch, Archie Stout (second-unit). Art director: Frank Hotaling. Set decorators: John McCarthy, Jr., Charles Thompson. Music: Victor Young. Songs, 'The Isle of Innisfree,' by Richard Farrelly; 'Galway Bay,' by Dr Arthur Colahan, Michael Donovan; 'The Humour Is On Me Now,' by Richard Hayward; 'The Young May Moon,' by Thomas Moore; and 'The Wild Colonel Boy,' 'Mush-Mush-Mush'. Editor: Jack Murray. Assistant editor: Barbara Ford. Second-unit directors (uncredited): John Wayne, Patrick Ford. Assistant director: Andrew McLaglen. Exteriors filmed in Ireland. 129 minutes. Released: September 14. With John Wayne (Sean Thornton), Maureen O'Hara (Mary Kate Danaher), Barry Fitzgerald (Michaeleen Og Flynn), Ward Bond (Father Peter Lonergan), Victor McLaglen (Red Will Danaher), Mildred Natwick (Mrs Sarah Tillane), Francis Ford (Dan Tobin), Eileen Crowe (Mrs Elizabeth Playfair), May Craig (woman at railroad station), Arthur Shields (Reverend Cyril Playfair), Charles FitzSimmons (Forbes), Sean McClory (Owen Glynn), James Lilburn (Father Paul), Jack McGowran (Feeney), Ken Curtis (Dermot Fahy), Mae Marsh (Father Paul's mother), Harry Tenbrook (policeman), Maj. Sam Harris (general), Joseph O'Dea (guard), Eric Gorman (railroad conductor), Kevin Lawless (fireman), Paddy O'Donnell (porter), Webb Overlander (railroad station clerk), Hank Worden (trainer in flashback), Harry Tyler (Pat Cohen), Don Hatswell (Guppy), David H. Hughes (constable), Douglas Evans (ring physician), Jack Roper (boxer), Al Murphy (referee), Patrick Wayne, Antonia Wayne, Melinda Wayne, Michael Wayne (children at race), Pat O'Malley, Bob Perry.

A retired American-Irish boxer returns to the land of his people: the picture Ford once called his 'first love story.' *Wayne and Pat Ford did several shots for the horse race sequence while Ford was ill; the picture won him his sixth Oscar, as well as one for its photography.*

1953 THE SUN SHINES BRIGHT (Republic). Director: John Ford. Producers: Ford, Merian C. Cooper. Scenarist: Laurence Stallings, from stories, 'The Sun Shines Bright,' 'The Mob from Massac,' 'The Lord Provides,' by Irvin S. Cobb. Photography: Archie Stout. Art director: Frank Hotaling. Set decorators: John McCarthy, Jr., George Milo. Costumes: Adele Palmer. Music: Victor Young. Editor: Jack Murray. Assistant editor: Barbara Ford. Assistant director: Wingate Smith. 90 minutes. Released: May 2. With Charles Winninger (Judge William Pittman Priest), Arleen Whelan (Lucy Lee Lake), John Russell (Ashby Corwin), Stepin' Fetchit (Jeff Poindexter), Russell Simpson (Dr. Lewt Lake), Ludwig Stossel (Herman Felsburg), Francis Ford (Feeney), Paul Hurst (Sgt Jimmy Bagby), Mitchell Lewis (Andy Redcliffe), Grant Withers (Buck Ramsey), Milburn Stone (Horace K. Maydew), Dorothy Jordan (Lucy's mother), Elzie Emanuel (U.S. Grant Woodford), Henry O'Neill (Jody Habersham), Slim Pickens (Sterling), James Kirkwood (Gen. Fairfield), Mae. Marsh (old lady at ball), Jane Darwell (Amora Ratchitt), Ernest Whitman (Uncle Pleasant Woodford), Trevor Bardette (Rufe, leader of lynch mob), Hal Baylor (his son), Eve March (Mallie Cramp), Clarence Muse (Uncle Zack), Jack Pennick (Beaker), Ken Williams, Patrick Wayne.

See *Judge Priest* (1934): even though it's election time in the 1905 Kentucky town, Judge Billy Priest still defends the unpopular case of a Negro accused of rape, and sees that the last wish of a prostitute is carried out.

1953 MOGAMBO (Metro–Goldwyn–Mayer). Director: John Ford. Producer: Sam Zimbalist. Scenarist: John Lee Mahin, from play, 'Red Dust,' by Wilson Collison. Photography (in color): Robert Surtees, Fredrick A. Young. Art director: Alfred Junge. Costumes: Helen Rose. Editor: Frank Clarke. Second-unit directors: Richard Rosson, Yakima Canutt, James C. Havens. Assistant directors: Wingate Smith, Cecil Ford. Exteriors filmed in Africa. 116 minutes. Released: October 9. With Clark Gable (Victor Marswell), Ava Gardner (Eloise Y. Kelly), Grace Kelly (Linda Nordley), Donald Sinden (Donald Nordley), Philip Stainton (John Brown Pryce), Eric Pohlmann (Leon Boltchak), Laurence Naismith (Skipper), Dennis O'Dea (Father Joseph), Asa Etula (young native girl), Wagenia Tribe of Belgian Congo, Samburu Tribe of Kenya Colony, Bahaya Tribe of Tanganyika, M'Beti Tribe of French Equatorial Africa.

During an African safari, a broad who's been around and a proper married lady both compete for the white hunter's attention. *A remake of Victor Fleming's* Red Dust (1932): *'I never saw the original picture,'* Ford said. *'I liked the script and the story, I liked the set-up and I'd never been to that part of Africa—so I just did it.'* (*In Vincente Minnelli's* The Courtship of Eddie's Father, 1963, *Glenn Ford watches a scene from* Mogambo *on T.V.*)

1953 *Hondo* (Wayne-Fellows–Warner Bros.). Director: John Farrow. Producer: Robert Fellows. Scenarist: James Edward Grant, from novel by Louis L'Amour. Photography (in color and 3-D): Robert Burks, Archie Stout. Second-unit director: Cliff Lyons and (uncredited) John Ford. Production manager: Andrew McLaglen. 83 minutes. Released: December. With John Wayne, Geraldine Page, Ward Bond, Michael Pate, James Arness.

Ford: 'I went down there to visit Duke, so immediately he sent me out to do some trivial second-unit stuff, a few stunts.'

1955 THE LONG GRAY LINE (Rota Productions–Columbia). Director: John Ford. Producer: Robert Arthur. Scenarist: Edward Hope, from autobiography, *Bringing Up the Brass*, by Marty Maher with Nardi Reeder Campion. Photography (in color and CinemaScope): Charles Lawton, Jr. Art director: Robert Peterson. Set decorator: Frank Tuttle. Music adaptation: George Duning. Editor: William Lyon. Assistant directors: Wingate Smith, Jack Corrick. 138 minutes. Released: February 9. With Tyrone Power (Martin Maher), Maureen O'Hara (Mary O'Donnell), Robert Francis (James Sundstrom, Jr.), Donald Crisp (Old Martin), Ward Bond (Capt. Herman J. Koehler), Betsy Palmer (Kitty Carter), Phil Carey (Charles Dotson), William Leslie (Red Sundstrom), Harry Carey, Jr. (Dwight Eisenhower), Patrick Wayne (Cherub Overton), Sean McClory (Dinny Maher), Peter Graves (Capt. Rudolph Heinz), Milburn Stone (Capt. John Pershing), Erin O'Brien-Moore (Mrs Koehler), Walter D. Ehlers (Mike Shannon), Don Barclay (Major Thomas), Martin Milner (Jim O'Carberry), Chuck Courtney (Whitey Larson), Willis Bouchey (doctor), Jack Pennick (sergeant).

Fifty years in the life of Marty Maher—and West Point. *Ford's first film in CinemaScope.*

1955 THE RED, WHITE AND BLUE LINE (U.S. Treasury Dept.-Columbia Pictures). Director: John Ford. Writer: Edward Hope. Photography (in color and CinemaScope): Charles Lawton, Jr. Narrator: Ward Bond. 10 minutes.

This promotional film urging Americans to buy savings bonds was made on the set of *The Long Gray Line* (1955) and features about 7 minutes from that picture.

141

1955 MISTER ROBERTS (Orange Productions–Warner Bros.).
Directors: John Ford, Mervyn LeRoy. Producer: Leland Hayward. Scenarists: Frank Nugent, Joshua Logan, from play by Logan, Thomas Heggen, and novel by Heggen. Photography (in color and CinemaScope): Winton C. Hoch. Art director: Art Loel. Set decorator: William L. Kuehl. Music: Franz Waxman. Editor: Jack Murray. Assistant director: Wingate Smith. Exteriors filmed in the Pacific. 123 minutes. Released: July 30. With Henry Fonda (Lt. [jg] Roberts), James Cagney (Captain), Jack Lemmon (Ensign Frank Thurlowe Pulver), William Powell (Doc), Ward Bond (C.P.O. Dowdy), Betsy Palmer (Lt. Ann Girard), Phil Carey (Mannion), Nick Adams (Reber), Harry Carey, Jr. (Stefanowski), Ken Curtis (Dolan), Frank Aletter (Gerhart), Fritz Ford (Lidstrom), Buck Kartalian (Mason), William Henry (Lt. Billings), William Hudson (Olson), Stubby Kruger (Schlemmer), Harry Tenbrook (Cookie), Perry Lopez (Rodrigues), Robert Roark (Insigna), Pat Wayne (Bookser), Tige Andrews (Wiley), Jim Moloney (Kennedy), Denny Niles (Gilbert), Francis Conner (Johnson) , Shug Fisher (Cochran), Danny Borzage (Jonesey), Jim Murphy (Taylor), Kathleen O'Malley, Maura Murphy, Mimi Doyle, Jeanne Murray-Vanderbilt, Lonnie Pierce (nurses), Martin Milner (shore patrol officer), Gregory Walcott (shore patrolman), James Flavin (M.P.), Jack Pennick (Marine sergeant), Duke Kahanamoko (native chief).

The story of a cargo ship in the Pacific during World War II. *Although Henry Fonda had played the title role on Broadway, Warners wanted either William Holden or Marlon Brando for the picture, on the premise that Fonda, who had been away from pictures since 1948 (Fort Apache), was no longer powerful at the box office. However, when Ford refused to do the film with anyone else, Fonda was signed for it. But, having played the role on stage for several years, Fonda had certain fixed ideas about the play and these began to clash with Ford's direction— he added a great deal of physical comedy in the exteriors and enlarged some of the minor roles. The arguments grew until, finally, according to Leland Hayward, a meeting that had been called to iron out the differences developed into an actual fistfight between Ford and Fonda. Shortly afterwards Ford got ill and LeRoy finished the picture (all the exteriors had been shot). Ford: 'I got a gall bladder attack towards the end of shooting, but I did most of the picture. A lot of that forced comedy inside the ship wasn't mine.'* (Lemmon received the Academy's Best Supporting Actor Award.)

1955 THE BAMBOO CROSS (Lewman Ltd.–Revue; episode for the *Fireside Theatre* television series).
Director: John Ford. Producer: William Asher. Scenarist: Laurence Stallings, from play by Theophane Lee. Photographer: John MacBurnie. Art director: Martin Obzina. Set decorator: James S. Redd. Music supervisor: Stanley Wilson. Supervising editor: Richard G. Wray. ˙Assistant director: Wingate Smith. Filmed November 7–11. 27 minutes. First broadcast: December 6. With Jane Wyman (Sister Regina), Betty Lynn (Sister Anne), Soo Yong (Sichi Sao), Jim Hong (Mark Chu), Judy Wong (Tanya), Don Summers (Ho Kwong), Kurt Katch (King Fat), Pat O'Malley (Priest), Frank Baker (bit man).

Two nuns in a Catholic convent in China are terrorized by a Communist overlord, who accuses them of having killed native babies; a Chinese boy sacrifices his life to help them escape. (*Interesting parallel with the story of* 7 Women, *made over ten years later.*)

1955 ROOKIE OF THE YEAR (Hal Roach Studios; episode for the *Screen Directors Playhouse* television series).
Director: John Ford. 29 minutes. First broadcast: December. With Pat Wayne (Lyn Goodhue), Vera Miles (Rose Goodhue), Ward Bond (Larry Goodhue, alias Buck Garrison), James Gleason (Ed), Willis Bouchey (newspaper editor), John Wayne (Mike, a reporter).

When it turns out that the father of baseball's newest rookie of the year was himself a champion rookie—who had become an alcoholic—a reporter refuses to write the story and the truth is never revealed.

1956 THE SEARCHERS (C. V. Whitney Pictures–Warner Bros.).
Director: John Ford. Producers: Merian C. Cooper, C. V. Whitney. Scenarist: Frank S. Nugent, from novel by Alan LeMay. Associate producer: Patrick Ford. Photography (in color and VistaVision): Winton C. Hoch, Alfred Gilks (second-unit). Art directors: Frank Hotaling, James Basevi. Set decorator: Victor Gangelin. Music: Max Steiner. Title song by Stan Jones. Editor: Jack Murray. Production supervisor: Lowell Farrell. Assistant director: Wingate Smith. Filmed in Colorado and in Monument Valley. 119 minutes. Released: May 26. With John Wayne (Ethan Edwards), Jeffrey Hunter (Martin Pawley), Vera Miles (Laurie Jorgensen), Ward Bond (Capt. Rev. Samuel Clayton), Natalie Wood (Debbie Edwards), John Qualen (Lars Jorgensen), Olive Carey (Mrs Jorgensen), Henry Brandon (Chief Scar), Ken Curtis (Charlie McCorry), Harry Carey, Jr. (Brad Jorgensen), Antonio Moreno (Emilio Figueroa), Hank Worden (Mose Harper), Lana Wood (Debbie as a child), Walter Coy (Aaron Edwards), Dorothy Jordan (Martha Edwards), Pippa Scott (Lucy Edwards), Pat Wayne (Lt. Green-

hill), Beulah Archuletta (Look), Jack Pennick (private), Peter Mamakos (Futterman), Bill Steele (Nesby), Cliff Lyons (Col. Greenhill), Chuck Roberson (man at wedding), Mae Marsh (woman at fort), Dan Borzage (accordionist at funeral), Billy Cartledge, Chuck Hayward, Slim Hightower, Fred Kennedy, Frank McGrath, Dale van Sickle, Henry Wills, Terry Wilson (stunt men), Away Luna, Billy Yellow, Bob Many Mules, Exactly Sonnie Betsuie, Feather Hat Jr., Harry Black Horse, Jack Tin Horn, Many Mules Son, Percy Shooting Star, Pete Grey Eyes, Pipe Line Begishe, Smile White Sheep (Comanches).

The ten-year search by two men for a little girl kidnapped by Comanches.

1957 THE WINGS OF EAGLES (Metro–Goldwyn–Mayer).

Director: John Ford. Producer: Charles Schnee. Associate producer: James E. Newcom. Scenarists: Frank Fenton, William Wister Haines, based on life and writings of Commander Frank W. Wead, USN. Art directors: William A. Horning, Malcolm Brown. Set decorators: Edwin B. Willis, Keogh Gleason. Costumes: Walter Plunket. Music: Jeff Alexander. Editor: Gene Ruggiero. Aerial stunts: Paul Mantz. Assistant director: Wingate Smith. 110 minutes. Released: February 22. With John Wayne (Frank W. 'Spig' Wead), Maureen O'Hara (Minne Wead), Dan Dailey (Carson), Ward Bond (John Dodge), Ken Curtis (John Dale Price), Edmund Lowe (Admiral Moffett), Kenneth Tobey (Herbert Allen Hazard), James Todd (Jack Travis), Barry Kelley (Capt. Jock Clark), Sig Ruman (manager), Henry O'Neill (Capt. Spear), Willis Bouchey (Barton), Dorothy Jordan (Rose Brentmann), Peter Ortiz (Lt. Charles Dexter), Louis Jean Heydt (Dr John Keye), Tige Andrews ('Arizona' Pincus), Dan Borzage (Pete), William Tracy (Air Force officer), Harlan Warde (Executive Officer), Jack Pennick (Joe), Bill Henry (Naval Aide), Alberto Morin (second manager), Mimi Gibson (Lila Wead), Evelyn Rudie (Doris Wead), Charles Trowbridge (Admiral Crown), Mae Marsh (Nurse Crumley), Janet Lake (nurse), Fred Graham (officer in brawl), Stuart Holmes (producer), Olive Carey (Bridy O'Faolain), Maj. Sam Harris (patient), May McEvoy (nurse), William Paul Lowery (Wead's baby, 'Commodore'), Chuck Roberson (officer), Cliff Lyons, Veda Ann Borg, Christopher James.

The story of 'Spig' Wead, an ace flier who turned to screenwriting when an accident left him paralyzed. *Wead* wrote Air Mail *and* They Were Expendable *for Ford and, among others, Howard Hawks'* Ceiling Zero (1936), *Frank Capra's* Dirigible (1931), *and George Hill's* Hell Divers (1932), *a clip from which is shown in* The Wings of Eagles.

1957 THE GROWLER STORY (U.S. Navy).

Director: John Ford. Producer: Mark Armistead. Photography (in 16mm. color): Pacific Fleet Combat Camera Group. Editor: Jack Murray. Assistant editor: Barbara Ford. Narrator: Dan Dailey. Shooting: November, 1956, in the Pacific. 29 minutes. With Ward Bond (Quincannon), Ken Curtis (Capt. Howard W. Gilmore), and Navy personnel, wives and children.

Made to publicize the Navy's submarine division, this short was based on a real World War II incident, in which a wounded Captain ordered his ship to submerge during an attack, leaving himself stranded on deck.

1957 THE RISING OF THE MOON (Four Province Productions–Warner Bros.).

Director: John Ford. Producer: Michael Killanin. Scenarist: Frank S. Nugent, from story, 'The Majesty of the Law,' by Frank O'Conner, and plays, 'A Minute's Wait,' by Michael J. McHugh, 'The Rising of the Moon,' by Lady Gregory. Photography: Robert Krasker. Art director: Ray Simm. Costumes: Jimmy Bourke. Music: Eamonn O'Gallagher. Editor: Michael Gordon. Filmed in Ireland. 81 minutes. Released: August 10. With (Introduction): Tyrone Power; (*The Majesty of the Law*): Noel Purcell (Dan O'Flaherty), Cyril Cusack (Inspector Michael Dillon), Jack McGowran (Mickey J.), Eric Gorman, Paul Farrell (neighbors), John Cowley (The Gombeen Man); (*A Minute's Wait*): Jimmy O'Dea (porter), Tony Quinn (railroad station chief), Paul Farrell (chauffeur), J. G. Devlin (guard), Michael Trubshawe (Col. Frobisher), Anita Sharp Bolster (Mrs Frobisher), Maureen Porter (barmaid), Godfrey Quigley (Christy), Harold Goldblatt (Christy's father), Maureen O'Connell (May Ann McMahon), May Craig (May's aunt), Michael O'Duffy (singer), Ann Dalton (fisherman's wife) Kevin Casey (Mr. McTigue); ('*1921*'): Dennis O'Dea (Police Sergeant), Eileen Crowe (his wife), Maurice Good (P.C. O'Grady), Frank Lawton (Major), Edward Lexy (R.Q.M.S.), Donal Donnelly (Sean Curran), Joseph O'Dea (chief of guards), Dennis Brennan, David Marlowe, Dennis Franks (English officers), Doreen Madden, Maureen Cusack (false nuns), Maureen Delaney (old woman), Martin Thornton (sergeant), John Horan (bill poster), Joe Hone, John Comeford, Mafra McDonagh (I.R.A. men), and members of the Abbey Theater Company.

Three Irish stories, in which: (1) a policeman visits a recalcitrant farmer; (2) a train that's supposed to stop for a minute, stops for two hours; (3) a young Irish-American patriot escapes during the 1921 rebellion. *Ford: 'I made it just for fun and enjoyed it very much.'*

1958 THE LAST HURRAH (Columbia).

Director-producer: John Ford. Scenarist: Frank Nugent, from novel by Edwin O'Conner. Photographer: Charles Lawton, Jr. Art director: Robert

Peterson. Set decorator: William Kiernan. Editor: Jack Murray. Assistant directors: Wingate Smith, Sam Nelson. 121 minutes. Released: November. With Spencer Tracy (Frank Skeffington), Jeffrey Hunter (Adam Caulfield), Dianne Foster (Maeve Caulfield), Pat O'Brien (John Gorman), Basil Rathbone (Norman Cass Sr.), Donald Crisp (the Cardinal), James Gleason (Cuke Gillen), Edward Brophy (Ditto Boland), John Carradine (Amos Force), Willis Bouchey (Roger Sugrue), Basil Ruysdael (Bishop Gardner), Ricardo Cortez (Sam Weinberg), Wallace Force (Charles J. Hennessey), Frank McHugh (Festus Garvey), Anna Lee (Gert Minihan), Jane Darwell (Delia Boylan), Frank Albertson (Jack Mangan), Charles FitzSimmons (Kevin McCluskey), Carleton Young (Mr Winslow), Bob Sweeney (Johnny Degnan), Edmund Lowe (Johnny Byrne), William Leslie (Dan Herlihy), Ken Curtis (Monseigneur Killian), O. Z. Whitehead (Norman Cass Jr.), Arthur Walsh (Frank Skeffington Jr.), Helen Westcott (Mrs McCluskey), Ruth Warren (Ellen Davin), Mimi Doyle (Mamie Burns), Dan Borzage (Pete), James Flavin (Police Captain), William Forrest (Doctor), Frank Sully (Fire Chief), Charlie Sullivan (chauffeur), Ruth Clifford (nurse), Jack Pennick (policeman), Richard Deacon (Plymouth Club Director), Harry Tenbrook, Eve March, Bill Henry, James Waters.

New England Mayor Frank Skeffington's glorious last campaign for re-election, which ends in defeat.

1959 GIDEON OF SCOTLAND YARD (GIDEON'S DAY) (Columbia British Productions–Columbia).

Director: John Ford. Producer: Michael Killanin. Associate producer: Wingate Smith. Scenarist: T. E. B. Clarke, from novel, *Gideon's Day*, by J. J. Marric (pseudonym for John Creasey). Photography (in color, but released in black and white): Frederick A. Young. Art director: Ken Adam. Music: Douglas Gamley. Editor: Raymond Poulton. Assistant director: Tom Pevsner. Filmed in London. 91 minutes. Released: February. With Jack Hawkins (Inspector George Gideon), Dianne Foster (Joanna Delafield), Anna Massey (Sally Gideon), Cyril Cusack (Herbert 'Birdie' Sparrow), Andrew Ray (P.C. Simon Farnaby-Green), James Hayter (Mason), Ronald Howard (Paul Delafield), Howard Marion-Crawford (Chief of Scotland Yard), Laurence Naismith (Arthur Sayer), Derek Bond (Det. Sgt Eric Kirby), Griselda Harvey (Mrs Kirby), Frank Lawton (Det. Sgt Liggott), Anna Lee (Mrs Kate Gideon), John Loder (Ponsford, 'The Duke'), Doreen Madden (Miss Courtney), Miles Malleson (Judge at Old Bailey), Marjorie Rhodes (Mrs Saparelli), Michael Shepley (Sir Rupert Bellamy), Michael Trubshawe (Sgt Golightly), Jack Watling

(Rev. Julian Small), Hermione Bell (Dolly Saparelli), Donal Donnelly (Feeney), Billie Whitelaw (Christine), Malcolm Ranson (Ronnie Gideon), Mavis Ranson (Jane Gideon), Francis Crowdy (Fitzhubert), David Aylmer (Manners), Brian Smith (White-Douglas), Barry Keegan (Riley, chauffeur), Maureen Potter (Ethel Sparrow), Henry Longhurst (Rev. Mr Courtney), Charles Maunsell (Walker), Stuart Saunders (Chancery Lane policeman), Dervis Ward (Simmo), Joan Ingram (Lady Bellamy), Nigel Fitzgerald (Insp. Cameron), Robert Raglan (Dawson), John Warwick (Insp. Gillick), John Le Mesurier (prosecuting attorney), Peter Godsell (Jimmy), Robert Bruce (defending attorney), Alan Rolfe (C.I.D. man at hospital), Derek Prentice (1st employer), Alastair Hunter (2nd employer), Helen Goss (woman employer), Susan Richmond (Aunt May), Raymond Rollett (Uncle Dick), Lucy Griffiths (cashier), Mary Donevan (usherette), O'Donovan Shiell, Bart Allison, Michael O'Duffy (policemen), Diana Chesney (barmaid), David Storm (court clerk), Gordon Harris (C.I.D. man).

One day in the life of Inspector Gideon, during which he deals with a dishonest associate, a mad killer, and a robbery—and receives two traffic tickets from a young bobby who, before the day is out, becomes his future son-in-law. *Ford: 'I wanted to get away for a while, so I said I'd like to do a Scotland Yard thing and we went over and did it.'*

1959 KOREA (U.S. Department of Defense).

Director: Rear Admiral John Ford, U.S.N.R. Producers: Ford, Capt. George O'Brien, U.S.N.(Retd.). Filmed in color in and around Seoul, Fall, 1958. 30 minutes. With O'Brien.

An orientation film on Korean history and customs, made specifically for American Occupation personnel.

1959 THE HORSE SOLDIERS (Mirisch Company–United Artists).

Director: John Ford. Producers-scenarists: John Lee Mahin, Martin Rackin, from novel by Harold Sinclair. Photography (in color): William H. Clothier. Art director: Frank Hotaling. Set decorator: Victor Gangelin. Music: David Buttolph. Song, 'I Left My Love,' by Stan Jones. Editor: Jack Murray. Assistant directors: Wingate Smith, Ray Gosnell, Jr. Filmed in Louisiana and in Mississippi. 119 minutes. Released: June. With John Wayne (Col. John Marlowe), William Holden (Maj. Hank Kendall), Constance Towers (Hannah Hunter), Althea Gibson (Lukey), Hoot Gibson (Brown), Anna Lee (Mrs Buford), Russell Simpson (Sheriff Capt. Henry Goodboy), Stan Jones (Gen. U.S. Grant),

144

Carleton Young (Col. Jonathan Miles), Basil Ruysdael (Commandant, Jefferson Military Academy), Willis Bouchey (Col. Phil Secord), Ken Curtis (Wilkie), O. Z. Whitehead ('Hoppy' Hopkins), Judson Pratt (Sgt Major Kirby), Denver Pyle (Jagger Jo), Strother Martin (Virgil), Hank Worden (Deacon), Walter Reed (Union officer), Jack Pennick (Sgt Major Mitchell), Fred Graham (Union soldier), Chuck Hayward (Union captain), Charles Seel (Newton Station bartender), Stuart Holmes, Maj. Sam Harris (passengers to Newton Station), Richard Cutting (Gen. Sherman), Bing Russell, William Forrest, William Leslie, Bill Henry, Ron Hagherty, Dan Borzage, Fred Kennedy.

In April, 1863, the U.S. Cavalry goes on a raid deep behind the Confederate lines; based on an actual Civil War mission.

1960 THE COLTER CRAVEN STORY (Revue Productions; episode from the *Wagon Train* television series).
Director: John Ford. Producer: Howard Christie. Writer: Tony Paulson. Photographer: Benjamin N. Kline. Art director: Martin Obzina. Set decorator: Ralph Sylos. Editors: Marston Fay, David O'Connell. 53 minutes. First broadcast: May. With Ward Bond (Maj. Seth Adams), Carleton Young (Colter Craven), Frank McGrath (Chuck Wooster), Terry Wilson (Bill Hawks), John Carradine (Park), Chuck Hayward (Quentin), Ken Curtis (Kyle), Anna Lee (Alarice Craven), Cliff Lyons (Creel), Paul Birch (Sam Grant), Annelle Hayes (Mrs Grant), Willis Bouchey (Jesse Grant), Mae Marsh (Mrs. Jesse Grant), Jack Pennick (drill sergeant), Hank Worden (Shelley), Charles Seel (Mort), Bill Henry (Krindle), Chuck Roberson (Junior), Dennis Rush (Jamie), Harry Tenbrook (Shelley's friend), Beulah Blaze, Lon Chaney, Jr., John Wayne (under pseudonym, Michael Morris, as Gen. Sherman).

His experiences at the Battle of Shiloh have left Dr Craven a drunken wreck. So that he will perform a necessary operation, Adams recounts the story of a disgraced alcoholic officer who had enough guts to make himself General of the Union Armies, and President of the United States—Ulysses Simpson Grant. *Footage from the river and the mountain crossing sequences from* Wagon Master—*the film which originally inspired the* Wagon Train *series—was used in this episode.* *Ford:* '*I've always wanted to do a feature on Grant—I think it's one of the great American stories—but you can't do it. You can't show him as a drunkard, but getting kicked out of the Army.*'

1960 SERGEANT RUTLEDGE (Ford Productions–Warner Bros.).
Director: John Ford. Producers: Patrick Ford, Willis Goldbeck. Writers: Goldbeck, James Warner Bellah. Photography (in color): Bert Glennon. Art director: Eddie Imazu. Set decorator: Frank M. Miller. Music: Howard Jackson. Song, 'Captain Buffalo,' by Mack David, Jerry Livingston. Editor: Jack Murray. Assistant directors: Russ Saunders, Wingate Smith. Filmed in Monument Valley. 111 minutes. Released: May. With Jeffrey Hunter (Lt. Tom Cantrell), Constance Towers (Mary Beecher), Woody Strode (Sgt Braxton Rutledge), Billie Burke (Mrs Cordelia Fosgate), Juano Hernandez (Sgt Matthew Luke Skidmore), Willis Bouchey (Col. Otis Fosgate), Carleton Young (Capt. Shattuck), Judson Pratt (Lt. Mulqueen), Bill Henry (Capt. Dwyer), Walter Reed (Capt. MacAfee), Chuck Hayward (Capt. Dickinson), Mae Marsh (Nellie), Fred Libby (Chandler Hubble), Toby Richards (Lucy Dabney), Jan Styne (Chris Hubble), Cliff Lyons (Sam Beecher), Charles Seel (Dr Eckner), Jack Pennick (sergeant), Hank Worden (Laredo), Chuck Roberson (juror), Eva Novak, Estelle Winwood (spectators), Shug Fisher (Mr Owens).

A young lieutenant in the 1880's defends a Negro sergeant unjustly accused of rape and murder. (Working title: *Captain Buffalo.*)

1960 *The Alamo* (Batjac–United Artists).
Director-producer: John Wayne. Writer: James Edward Grant. Photography (in color and Todd-AO): William H. Clothier. Second-unit director: Cliff Lyons (and uncredited: John Ford). Technical supervisors: Jack Pennick, Frank Beetson. 190 minutes. Released: October. With John Wayne, Richard Widmark, Laurence Harvey, Richard Boone, Frankie Avalon, Patrick Wayne, Chill Wills, Linda Cristal, Ken Curtis.

Ford: 'I was merely down there on vacation and Duke said, "Do you mind going out and getting a shot of so-and-so?" And I did. We got some wonderful scenes—guys swimming rivers, that sort of thing—but they were all cut out.'

1961 TWO RODE TOGETHER (Ford–Shpetner Productions–Columbia).
Director: John Ford. Producer: Stan Shpetner. Scenarist: Frank Nugent, from novel, *Comanche Captives,* by Will Cook. Photography (in color): Charles Lawton, Jr. Art director: Robert Peterson. Set decorator: James M. Crowe. Music: George Duning. Editor: Jack Murray. Assistant director: Wingate Smith. Filmed in Southwest Texas. 109

minutes. Released: July. With James Stewart (Guthrie McCabe), Richard Widmark (Lt. Jim Gary), Shirley Jones (Marty Purcell), Linda Cristal (Elena de la Madriaga), Andy Devine (Sgt Darius P. Posey), John McIntire (Maj. Frazer), Paul Birch (Edward Purcell), Willis Bouchey (Harry J. Wringle), Henry Brandon (Quanah Parker), Harry Carey, Jr. (Ortho Clegg), Ken Curtis (Greely Clegg), Olive Carey (Abby Frazer), Chet Douglas (Ward Corbey), Annelle Hayes (Belle Aragon), David Kent (Running Wolf), Anna Lee (Mrs Malaprop), Jeanette Nolan (Mrs McCandless), John Qualen (Ole Knudsen), Ford Rainey (Henry Clegg), Woody Strode (Stone Calf), O. Z. Whitehead (Lt. Chase), Cliff Lyons (William McCandless), Mae Marsh (Hannah Clegg), Frank Baker (Capt. Malaprop), Ruth Clifford (woman), Ted Knight (Lt. Upton), Maj. Sam Harris (post doctor), Jack Pennick (sergeant), Chuck Roberson (Comanche), Dan Borzage, Bill Henry, Chuck Hayward, Edward Brophy.

A cynical sheriff and a cavalry lieutenant ride into Comanche territory to trade for some white children who were kidnapped years before.

1962 THE MAN WHO SHOT LIBERTY VALANCE (Ford Productions–Paramount).

Director: John Ford. Producer: Willis Goldbeck. Scenarists: Goldbeck, James Warner Bellah, from story by Dorothy M. Johnson. Photography: William H. Clothier. Art directors: Hal Pereira, Eddie Imazu. Set decorators: Sam Comer, Darrell Silvera. Costumes: Edith Head. Music: Cyril J. Mockridge; theme from *Young Mr Lincoln*, by Alfred Newman. Editor: Otho Lovering. Assistant director: Wingate Smith. 122 minutes. Released: April. With James Stewart (Ransom Stoddard), John Wayne (Tom Doniphon), Vera Miles (Hallie Stoddard), Lee Marvin (Liberty Valance), Edmond O'Brien (Dutton Peabody), Andy Devine (Link Appleyard), Ken Murray (Doc Willoughby), John Carradine (Starbuckle), Jeanette Nolan (Nora Ericson), John Qualen (Peter Ericson), Willis Bouchey (Jason Tully), Carleton Young (Maxwell Scott), Woody Strode (Pompey), Denver Pyle (Amos Carruthers), Strother *Martin* (Floyd), Lee Van Cleef (Reese), Robert F. Simon (Handy Strong), O. Z. Whitehead (Ben Carruthers), Paul Birch (Mayor Winder), Joseph Hoover (Hasbrouck), Jack Pennick (barman), Anna Lee (passenger), Charles Seel (President, Election Council), Shug Fisher (drunk), Earle Hodgins, Stuart Holmes, Dorothy Phillips, Buddy Roosevelt, Gertrude Astor, Eva Novak, Slim Talbot, Monty Montana, Bill Henry, John B. Whiteford, Helen Gibson, Maj. Sam Harris.

Senator Ransom Stoddard returns to Shinbone for the funeral of a pauper and tells an enquiring reporter the true story of who shot Liberty Valance.

1962 FLASHING SPIKES (Avista Productions–Revue; episode for the *Alcoa Premiere* television series).

Director: John Ford. Associate producer: Frank Baur. Scenarist: Jameson Brewer, from novel by Frank O'Rourke. Photographer: William H. Clothier. Art director: Martin Obzina. Set decorators: John McCarthy, Martin C. Bradfield. Music: Johnny Williams. Editors: Richard Belding, Tony Martinelli. Titles: Saul Bass. Series host: Fred Astaire. 53 minutes. First broadcast: October 4. With James Stewart (Slim Conway), Jack Warden (Commissioner), Pat Wayne (Bill Riley), Edgar Buchanan (Crab Holcomb), Tige Andrews (Gaby Lasalle), Carleton Young (Rex Short), Willis Bouchey (mayor), Don Drysdale (Gomer), Stephanie Hill (Mary Riley), Charles Seel (judge), Bing Russell (Hogan), Harry Carey, Jr. (man in dugout), Vin Scully (announcer), Walter Reed (second reporter), Sally Hughes (nurse), Larry Blake (first reporter), Charles Morton (umpire), Cy Malis (the bit man), Bill Henry (Commissioner's assistant), John Wayne (drill sergeant in Korea), Art Passarella (umpire), Vern Stephens, Ralph Volkie, Earl Gilpin, Bud Harden, Whitey Campbell (baseball players).

Still hanging around the training grounds, an old ballplayer whose career was ruined by a bribery scandal, strikes up a friendship with a young first baseman, who helps to clear his name.

1962 *How The West Was Won* (Cinerama–Metro–Goldwyn–Mayer).

Directors: John Ford (The Civil War), George Marshall (The Railroad), Henry Hathaway (The Rivers, The Plains, The Outlaws). Producer: Bernard Smith. Scenarist: James R. Webb, suggested by series in *Life*. Art directors: George W. Davis, William Ferrari, Addison Hehr. Set decorators: Henry Grace, Don Greenwood, Jr, Jack Mills. Music: Alfred Newman, Ken Darby. Editor: Harold F. Kress. Narrator: Spencer Tracy. 162 minutes. Released: November. *For the Ford sequence:* Photography (in color, Cinerama and Ultra Panavision): Joseph La Shelle. Assistant director: Wingate Smith. 15 minutes. With John Wayne (Gen. William T. Sherman), George Peppard (Zeb Rawlings), Carroll Baker (Eve Prescott), Henry (Harry) Morgan (Gen. U. S. Grant), Andy Devine (Corporal Peterson), Russ Tamblyn (deserter), Willis Bouchey (surgeon), Claude Johnson (Jeremiah Rawlings), Raymond Massey (Abraham Lincoln).

Ford's brief sequence—the one bright spot in an otherwise dreary film (his first work in Cinerama)—told of the Battle of Shiloh, perhaps the bloodiest encounter in the Civil War, and of the tragic home-comings that followed.

1963 DONOVAN'S REEF (Ford Productions–Paramount).
Director-producer: John Ford. Scenarists: Frank Nugent, James Edward Grant, from story by Edmund Beloin, adapted by James Michener. Photography (in color): William Clothier. Art directors: Hal Pereira, Eddie Imazu. Set decorators: Sam Comer, Darrell Silvera. Costumes: Edith Head. Music: Cyril J. Mockridge. Editor: Otho Lovering. Assistant director: Wingate Smith. Filmed on the island of Kauai in the South Pacific. 109 minutes. Released: July. With John Wayne (Michael Patrick 'Guns' Donovan), Lee Marvin (Thomas Aloysius 'Boats' Gilhooley), Elizabeth Allen (Amelia Sarah Dedham), Jack Warden (Dr William Dedham), Cesar Romero (Marquis Andre De Lage), Dorothy Lamour (Miss Lafleur), Jacqueline Malouf (Lelani Dedham), Mike Mazurki (Sgt Menkowicz), Marcel Dalio (Father Cluzeot), Jon Fong (Mister Eu), Cheryline Lee (Sally Dedham), Tim Stafford (Luki Dedham), Carmen Estrabeau (Sister Gabrielle), Yvonne Peattie (Sister Matthew), Frank Baker (Captain Martin), Edgar Buchanan (Boston Notary), Pat Wayne (Navy lieutenant), Charles Seel (Grand Uncle Sedley Atterbury), Chuck Roberson (Festus), Mae Marsh, Maj. Sam Harris (Members of Family Counsel), Dick Foran, Cliff Lyons (Officers), and Ford's yacht, The Araner.
A couple of Navy men who have retired to a South Seas Island now spend most of their time raising hell.

1964 CHEYENNE AUTUMN (Ford–Smith Productions–Warner Bros.).
Director: John Ford. Producer: Bernard Smith. Scenarist: James R. Webb, from book by Mari Sandoz. Photography (in color and Panavision): William Clothier. Art director: Richard Day. Set decorator: Darrell Silvera. Associate director: Ray Kellogg. Music: Alex North. Editor: Otho Lovering. Sound editor: Francis E. Stahl. Assistant directors: Wingate Smith, Russ Saunders. Filmed in Monument Valley; Moab, Utah; Gunnison, Colorado. 159 minutes. Released: October. With Richard Widmark (Capt. Thomas Archer), Carroll Baker (Deborah Wright), James Stewart (Wyatt Earp), Edward G. Robinson, (Secretary of the Interior Carl Schurz), Karl Malden (Capt. Wessels), Sal Mineo (Red Shirt), Dolores Del Rio (Spanish Woman), Ricardo Montalban (Little Wolf), Gilbert Roland (Dull Knife), Arthur Kennedy (Doc Holliday), Patrick Wayne (2nd Lieut. Scott), Elizabeth Allen (Guinevere Plantagenet), John Carradine (Maj. Jeff Blair), Victor Jory (Tall Tree), Mike Mazurki

(Top Sergeant Stanislas Wichowsky), George O'Brien (Maj Braden), Sean McClory (Dr O'Carberry), Judson Pratt (Mayor 'Dog' Kelly), Carmen D'Antonio (Pawnee Woman), Ken Curtis (Joe), Walter Baldwin (Jeremy Wright), Shug Fisher (Skinny), Nancy Hsueh (Little Bird), Chuck Roberson (Platoon Sergeant), Harry Carey, Jr. (Trooper Smith), Ben Johnson (Trooper Plumtree), Jimmy O'Hara (Trooper), Chuck Hayward (Trooper), Lee Bradley (Cheyenne), Frank Bradley (Cheyenne), Walter Reed (Lt. Peterson), Willis Bouchey (Colonel), Carleton Young (Aide to Carl Schurz), Denver Pyle (Senator Henry), John Qualen (Svenson), Nanomba 'Moonbeam' Morton (Running Deer), Dan Borzage, Dean Smith, David H. Miller, Bing Russell (Troopers).
The tragic flight of 286 Cheyenne men, women and children, pursued by the Cavalry from a barren Oklahoma reservation to their native Yellowstone country 1,800 miles away. (Working title: *The Long Flight*.

1965 *Young Cassidy* (Sextant Films-Metro-Goldwyn-Mayer).
Directors: Jack Cardiff, John Ford (official credit: 'A John Ford Film'). Producers: Robert D. Graff, Robert Emmett Ginna. Associate producer: Michael Killanin. Scenarist: John Whiting, from autobiography, *Mirror in My House*, by Sean O'Casey. Photography (in color): Ted Scaife. Art director: Michael Stringer. Costumes: Margaret Furse. Music: Sean O'Riada. Editor: Anne V. Coates. Filmed in Ireland. 110 minutes. Released: March. With Rod Taylor (Sean Cassidy), Maggie Smith (Nora), Julie Christie (Daisy Battles), Flora Robson (Mrs Cassidy), Sian Phillips (Ella), Michael Redgrave (William Butler Yeats), Dame Edith Evans (Lady Gregory), Jack MacGowran (Archie), T. P. McKenna (Tom), Julie Ross (Sara), Robin Sumner (Michael), Philip O'Flynn (Mick Mullen), Pauline Delaney (Bessie Ballynoy), Arthur O'Sullivan (foreman), Tom Irwin (constable), John Cowley (barman), William Foley (publisher's clerk), John Franklyn (bank teller), Harry Brogan (Murphy), James Fitzgerald (Charlie Ballynoy), Donal Donnelly (undertaker's man), Harold Goldblatt (Director of Abbey Theatre), Ronald Ibbs (theatre employee), May Craig, May Cluskey (women in the hall), Tom Irwin, Shivaun O'Casey, and members of the Abbey Theatre.
Ford prepared this film about Sean O'Casey's early years, and when he became ill (shortly after the start of production), the producers announced that Jack Cardiff would follow Ford's design for the rest of the shooting. Ford: 'I only did a few day's work—some scenes between Julie [Christie] and Rod Taylor.'

1966   7 WOMEN (Ford-Smith Productions-Metro-Goldwyn-Mayer).
Director: John Ford. Producer: Bernard Smith. Scenarists: Janet Green, John McCormick, from story, 'Chinese Finale,' by Norah Lofts. Photography (in color and Panavision): Joseph LaShelle. Art directors: George W. Davis, Eddie Imazu. Set decorators: Henry Grace, Jack Mills. Costumes: Walter Plunkett. Music: Elmer Bernstein. Editor: Otho S. Lovering. Assistant director: Wingate Smith. 87 minutes. Released: January. With Anne Bancroft (Dr D. R. Cartwright), Sue Lyon (Emma Clark), Margaret Leighton (Agatha Andrews), Flora Robson (Miss Binns), Mildred Dunnock (Jane Argent), Betty Field (Florrie Pether), Anna Lee (Mrs′ Russell), Eddie Albert (Charles Pether), Mike Mazurki (Tunga Khan), Woody Strode (Lean Warrior), Jane Chang (Miss Ling), Hans William Lee (Kim), H. W. Gim (Coolie), Irene Tsu (Chinese girl).

In 1935, a doctor sacrifices herself to save the lives of a group of missionaries held captive by a Chinese warlord. (*Anne Bancroft replaced Patricia Neal who was taken ill after three days of shooting.*)

UNREALIZED PROJECTS

1965–66 *The Miracle of Merriford* (unrealized project). Ford was signed by MGM to make this film version of Reginald Arkell's novel about a small English town in World War II, whose church is damaged by American forces moving in their equipment. The bulk of the story dealt with the conflicts between American and British temperament, as two G.I.'s (one of whom was to have been played by Dan Dailey) try to raise the money to pay for repairs. The script, by Willis Goldbeck and James Warner Bellah, was turned down by the studio and the project was shelved. According to Ford, it was to have been a film in the same vein as *The Quiet Man;* he was very pleased with the screenplay.

1967–68 *April Morning* (unrealized). A screenplay by Michael Wilson, to have been produced by Samuel Goldwyn, Jr. Ford: 'It's the story of a blacksmith and his family just before the Revolutionary War. The Battle of Lexington and Concord will be in the film—we'll have the fight and the retreat—but basically it's the story of a father and his son. There have been very few pictures about the American Revolution—I think because actors are afraid of wearing those wigs. But the people in the country—most of them—didn't go to all that trouble—so in this picture, the lead doesn't have to wear a wig.'

1967–68 *O.S.S.* (unrealized). The story of the World War II intelligence agency, and of the man who was its chief (and

Ford's friend), Major General William J. ('Wild Bill') Donovan, was to have been played probably by John Wayne.

1969–73 *Valley Forge,* a Revolutionary War epic to have been co-produced with Frank Capra; *The White Company,* from the famous novel; *The Josh Clayton Story,* about the black soldier, to have starred Fred Williamson. These were all projects to which Ford gave his attention in his last years, none of them realized.

1971 *Directed by John Ford* (California Arts Commission-American Film Institute).
Director-Writer-Interviewer: Peter Bogdanovich. Producers: George Stevens, Jr., and James R. Silke. Interview Photography (in color): Laszlo Kovacs, Gregory Sandor, Brick Marquard, Eric Sherman. Editor: Richard Patterson. Assistant to Director: Mae Woods. Associate Producer: David Shepard. Narrator: Orson Welles. 95 minutes. First shown: 32nd Venice Film Festival, Sept. 15, at which time Ford was there to receive the Festival's highest award. With John Ford, John Wayne, Henry Fonda, James Stewart.

Filmed interviews with actors who had worked with Ford and with the director himself at Monument Valley, reluctantly talking about his work, interspersed with clips from 27 of his pictures. (Available in 16 mm. through Films, Inc.)

1971 *The American West of John Ford* (Group One-Timex-CBS).
Director: Denis Sanders. Executive Producer: Bob Banner. Producers: Tom Egan, Britt Lomond, Dan Ford. Writer: David H. Vowell. Photographer: Bob Collins. Editor: Keith Olson. First broadcast: December 5. With John Ford, John Wayne, James Stewart, Henry Fonda.

Documentary included clips from Ford Westerns (1917–1962); the director appeared with John Wayne in Monument Valley where he directed a stunt; interview footage with James Stewart and Henry Fonda was shot at Ford's home in Bel Air, and additional material with Fonda was shot overlooking the old Fox lot in Century City.

1972 *Vietnam! Vietnam!* (U.S.I.A.).
Director: Sherman Beck. Executive Producer: John Ford. Producer: Bruce Herschensohn. 58 minutes.

Though completed, this government documentary was never distributed.

1973 *The American Film Institute First Annual Life Achievement Award* (CBS).
Producer: George Stevens, Jr.

President Nixon also appeared to present Ford the Civilian Medal of Honor. John Wayne, Maureen O'Hara, Danny Kaye and many others performed for the evening, taped on March 31 and first shown on television on April 2.

1974 *JOHN FORD: Memorial Day 1970.*
Director-Writer-Editor: Mark Haggard. Producers: Haggard,

Paul Magwood, Lowell Peterson. Photographer: Douglas Knapp. Narrator: Linda Strawn. 12 minutes. First shown: April. With John Ford, Walter Pidgeon, Anna Lee, Harry Carey, Jr., Olive Carey, Dan Borzage, Dick Amador, Meta Sterne, George Bagnall, Ray Kellogg, Mary Ford, Wingate Smith.

Documentary features the members of John Ford's Field Photo Unit at the 24th Annual Memorial Day Services at the Motion Picture Country Home in Woodland Hills, California.

1976 *CHESTY* (James Ellsworth Productions).

Director: John Ford. Producer: James Ellsworth. Writer: Jay Simms. Photography: Brick Marquard. Music: Jack Marshall. Editor-Associate Producer: Leon Selditz. Assistant to Producer: Charles C. Townsend. 28 minutes. First shown: April 4 (Filmex, Los Angeles). Host: John Wayne.

Documentary about Lt. General Lewis "Chesty" Puller, USMC, shot at his home in Saluda, Virginia, includes visits with him to the Stonewall Jackson Monument and Robert E. Lee's tomb, plus locations at Camp Pendleton, Virginia Military Institute and the Marine Barracks in Washington, D.C., as well as footage from Ford's own *This Is Korea!* John Wayne's commentary was shot on the set of Rio Lobo in Tucson, Arizona. Shooting began in August, 1968, and was finished in Tucson on April 8, 1970. The original 60 minute version was edited for possible television sale; Ford is said to have preferred the shorter cut.

SELECTED BIBLIOGRAPHY

Cahiers du Cinéma, in *Special John Ford* (No. 183, 1966), filmography, interview, two articles; in issue No. 45 (March 1955), an interview.

Films in Review, in March 1963 issue, 'The Films of John Ford,' a filmography; in June–July 1964 issue, 'Ford on Ford,' report of a UCLA symposium.

Gassner, John and Nichols, Dudley (eds.), in *Twenty Best Film Plays* (Crown, 1943), complete scenarios of 'Stagecoach,' 'The Grapes of Wrath,' 'How Green Was My Valley.'

Kezich, Tullio, *John Ford* (Guandra, 1958).

McBride, Joseph and Wilmington, Michael, *John Ford* (Secker & Warburg, Ltd., 1974, and Da Capo Press, 1975).

Miller, Arthur C. and Balshofer, Fred J., in *One Reel a Week* (University of California Press, 1967), several chapters on working with Ford.

Mitry, Jean, *John Ford* (two volumes; Editions Universitaires, 1954, reprinted in one volume in 1964).

Présence du Cinéma, in *John Ford Issue* (No. 21, 1965), filmography and four articles.

Sarris, Andrew, *The John Ford Movie Mystery* (Indiana University Press, 1976).

Sequence, in issue No. 14 (1952), an interview.

Theatre Arts, in *Hollywood Issue* (August 1951), complete scenario of 'The Informer'.

Wooten, William Patrick, *An Index to the Films of John Ford* (Sight and Sound Supplement, Index Series No. 13, 1948).